Project Management:
Practical Tools for Success

Project Management: Practical Tools for Success

Mona Abid

MD Publications Pvt Ltd
New Delhi

Published by
MD Publications Pvt Ltd
"MD House", 11, Darya Ganj
New Delhi-110002
Tel. : +91-11-41563325, 41562846
E-mail : contact@mdppl.com
Website : www.mdppl.com

ISBN: 978-81-7533-113-6

PRICE: Rs. 995.00

Published and Printed by **MD Publications Pvt Ltd** at Times Press, 910, Jatwara Street, Darya Ganj, New Delhi.

Contents

Preface

Project management is the discipline of organizing and managing resources in such a way that the project is completed within defined scope, quality, time and cost constraints. A project is a temporary and one-time endeavor undertaken to create a unique product or service, which brings about beneficial change or added value. This property of being a temporary and one-time undertaking contrasts with processes, or operations, which are permanent or semi-permanent ongoing functional work to create the same product or service over and over again. The management of these two systems is often very different and requires varying technical skills and philosophy, hence requiring the development of project management.

The first challenge of project management is to make sure that a project is delivered within defined constraints. The second, more ambitious challenge is the optimized allocation and integration of inputs needed to meet pre-defined objectives. A project is a carefully defined set of activities that use resources (money, people, materials, energy, space, provisions, communication, etc.) to meet the pre-defined objectives.

Project management is quite often the province and responsibility of an individual project manager. This individual seldom participates directly in the activities that produce the end result, but rather strives to maintain the progress and productive mutual interaction of various parties in such a way that overall risk of failure is reduced.

A project manager is often a client representative and has to determine and implement the exact needs of the client, based on knowledge of the firm he/she is representing. The ability to adapt to the various internal procedures of the contracting party, and to form close links with the nominated representatives, is essential in ensuring that the key issues of cost, time, quality, and above all, client satisfaction, can be realized.

Customers either internal or external project sponsors and external organizations (such as government agencies and regulators) can dictate the extent of three variables: time, cost, and scope. The remaining variable (risk) is managed by the project team, ideally based on solid estimation and response planning techniques. Through a negotiation process among project stakeholders, an agreement defines the final objectives, in terms of time, cost, scope, and risk, usually in the form of a charter or contract.

There are several approaches that can be taken to managing project activities including agile, interactive, incremental, and phased approaches. Regardless of the approach employed, careful consideration needs to be given to clarify surrounding project objectives, goals, and importantly, the roles and responsibilities of all participants and stakeholders.

Thanks to Mr. Pranav Gupta of **MD Publications Pvt Ltd**, New Delhi, who supported me fully for completing this book.

Mona Abid

1

Project Management: Definition and Meaning

Introduction

Project management is the process of managing, allocating, and timing resources to achieve a given goal in an efficient and expedient manner. The objectives that constitute the specified goal may be in terms of time, costs, or technical results. A project can be quite simple or very complex. An example of a simple project is painting a small, vacant room. An example of a complex project is launching a space shuttle.

Project management techniques are used widely in many enterprises, including construction, banking, manufacturing, marketing, health care services, transportation, R&D, public services, and so on. The standard hierarchy of the elements of project consists of system, program, project, task, and activity.

System: A project system consists of interrelated elements organized for the purpose of achieving a common goal. The elements are expected to work synergistically together to generate a unified output that is greater than the sum of the individual outputs of the components.

Program: A program is a very large and prolonged undertaking. Typically, such project endeavors span several years. Programs are usually associated with particular systems, for example, a space exploration program within a national defense system.

Project: A project is a time-phased effort of much smaller scope and duration than a program. Programs are sometimes viewed as consisting of a set of projects, but practitioners often refer to both without distinction. Government projects are often called *programs* because of their broad and comprehensive nature. The industrial sector, on the other hand, tends to use the term *project* because of the short-term and focused nature of most industrial efforts.

Task: A task is a functional element of a project. A project is normally composed of contiguous arrays of tasks that all contribute to the overall project goal.

Activity: An activity can be defined as a single element of a project. Activities are generally smaller in scope than tasks. In a detailed analysis of a project, an activity may be viewed as the smallest, practically indivisible work element of the project. For example, we can regard a manufacturing plant as a system. A plant-wide endeavor to improve productivity can be viewed as a program. The installation of a flexible manufacturing system is a project within the productivity improvement program. The process of identifying and selecting equipment vendors is a task, and the actual process of placing an order with a preferred vendor is an activity. Figure 1.1 presents the functional and hierarchical relationships between the components of a project.

The techniques of project management can help achieve goals relating to better product quality, improved resource utilization, better customer relations, higher productivity, and fulfillment of due dates. These can generally be expressed in terms of the following project constraints:

- Performance Specifications
- Schedule Requirements
- Cost Limitations

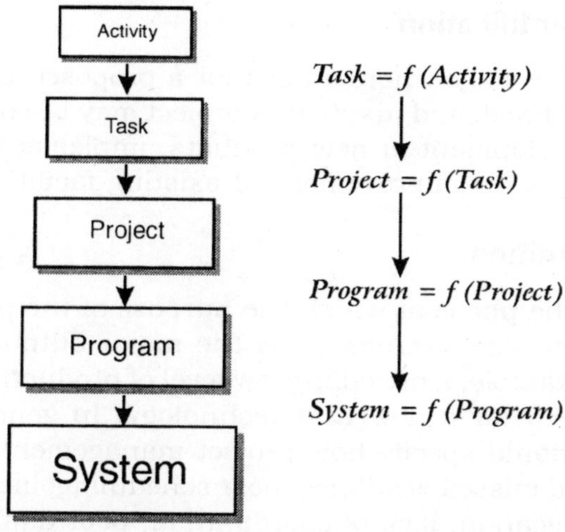

Figure 1.1. Hierarchy of Project Components

Steps of Project Management

Figure 1.2 presents the major steps in project management. The life cycle of a project typically consists of several steps going from problem identification, definition, planning (specifications and project formulation), organizing, resource allocation, scheduling, tracking and reporting, and control to project termination. The steps are typically performed strategically in accordance with the specified project goal. These steps are discussed briefly below; some are discussed in further detail in subsequent sections.

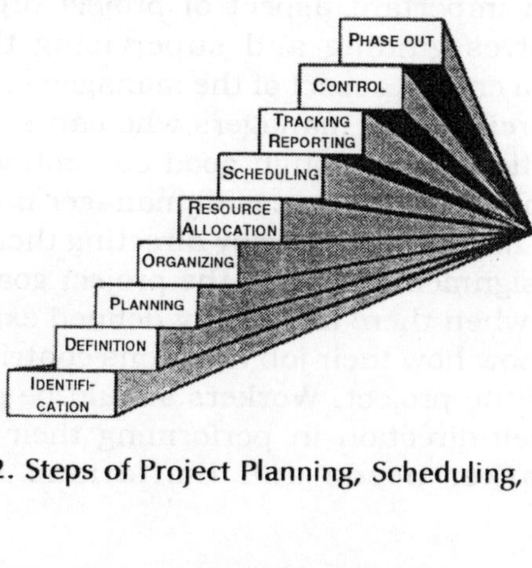

Figure 1.2. Steps of Project Planning, Scheduling, and Control

Problem Identification

This is the stage where a need for a proposed project is identified, defined, and justified. A project may be concerned with the development of new products, implementation of new processes, or improvement of existing facilities.

Project Definition

This is the phase at which the purpose of the project is clarified. A mission statement is the major output of this stage. For example, a prevailing low level of productivity may trigger a need for a new CIM technology. In general, the definition should specify how project management may be used to avoid missed deadlines, poor scheduling, inadequate resource allocation, lack of coordination, poor quality, and conflicting priorities.

Project Planning

Project planning determines how to initiate a project and execute its objectives. Because of its need for extensive coverage in project management.

Project Organizing

Project organization specifies how to integrate the functions of the personnel involved in a project. Organizing is normally done concurrently with project planning. Directing is an important aspect of project organization. Directing involves guiding and supervising the project personnel. It is a crucial aspect of the management function. Directing requires skillful managers who can interact with subordinates effectively through good communication and motivation techniques. A successful manager improves the performance of his subordinates by directing them, through proper task assignments, toward the project goal. Workers perform better when there are clearly defined expectations. They need to know how their job functions contribute to the overall goals of the project. Workers should be given some flexibility for self-direction in performing their functions. Individual worker needs and limitations should be recognized by the manager when directing project functions. Project directing consists of the following elements:

Approach: Development of a method of approach (communication or otherwise) to subordinates at various levels and in different situations.

Supervising: Monitoring, guiding, and reviewing of the day-to-day activities of subordinates with respect to the project goal.

Delegating: Assignment of responsibility or secondary authority to subordinates for the execution of certain functions so as to enhance the utilization of manpower resources.

Motivating: Boosting the morale and interest of subordinates in performing their jobs. This requires understanding the needs, motives, and feelings of subordinates and an appreciation for the nature of their responses to certain directives.

Resource Allocation

Project goals and objectives are accomplished by applying resources to functional requirements. Resources, in the context of project management, are generally made up of people and equipment, which are typically in short supply. The people needed for a particular task may be committed to other ongoing projects. A crucial piece of equipment may be under the control of a competitor.

Project Scheduling

Scheduling is often recognized as the major function in project management. The main purpose of scheduling is to allocate resources so that the overall project objectives are achieved within a reasonable time span. In general, scheduling involves the assignment of time periods to specific tasks within the work schedule. Resource availability, time limitations, urgency level, required performance level, precedence requirements, work priorities, technical constraints, and other factors complicate the scheduling process. Thus, the assignment of a time slot to a task does not necessarily ensure that the task will be performed satisfactorily in accordance with the schedule. Consequently, careful control must be developed and maintained throughout the project scheduling process. A separate section of this chapter is devoted to further discussion of project scheduling. Many of the quantitative models presented in this book relate to achieving better project schedules.

Project Tracking and Reporting

This phase involves the process of checking whether or not project results conform to plans and specifications. Tracking and reporting are prerequisites for project control. A properly organized report of the project status will quickly identify the deficiencies in the progress of the project and help pinpoint necessary corrective actions.

Project Control

In this function, necessary actions are taken to correct unacceptable deviations from expected performance. Control is effected by measurement, evaluation, and corrective action. Measurement is the process of measuring the relationship between planned performance and actual performance with respect to project objectives. The variables to be measured, the measurement scales, and the measuring approaches should be clearly specified during the planning stage.

Project Phase Out

This is the last stage of a project. The phase out is as important as the initiation. The termination of a project should be implemented expeditiously. A project should not be allowed to drag on after the expected completion time. A terminal activity should be defined for a project during the planning phase. An example of a terminal activity may be the submission of a final report, the "power-on" of new equipment, or the signing of a release order. The conclusion of such an activity should be viewed as the completion of the project. To prevent a project from dragging on needlessly, strict directives should be issued about when it will end. However, provisions should be made for follow-up activities that may improve the results of the project. These follow-up or spin-off projects should be managed as totally separate projects but with proper input-output relationships within the sequence of projects. If a project is not terminated when appropriate, the motivation for it will wane and subsequent activities may become counterproductive. This is particularly tree for technology-based projects where the "fear of the unknown" and "resistance to change" are already major obstacles.

Project Organization Structures

Project organization structures may be selected on the basis of functional specializations, departmental proximity, standard management boundaries, organizational policies, operational relationships, or product requirements.

Formal and Informal Organization

A formal organization is an officially sanctioned structure within an organization. An informal organization develops when people organize in an unofficial way to accomplish an objective that is in line with the overall project goal. Such an informal organization is often very subtle in that not everyone in the general organization is aware of its existence. Even some of those who are aware of its existence may not be welcome to participate in it Friends and close associates often organize informally to pursue project goals. Both formal and informal modes of organization are practiced in any organization, even those that have strict hierarchical structures, such as the military.

Functional Organization

Projects that are organized along functional lines are normally found in some departmental area of specialization. That is, the project is located in a specific department. For example, projects that involve manufacturing operations may be under the direction of the vice-president of manufacturing, while a project involving new technology may be assigned to the technology development department. Functional organization is the most common type of formal organization. The advantages of functional organization are:

- ❒ Flexibility in manpower utilization
- ❒ Improved productivity of specially skilled personnel
- ❒ Enhanced comradeship of technical staff
- ❒ Potential for staff advancement along functional lines
- ❒ Improved accountability
- ❒ Clear lines of control

The disadvantages of functional organization are:

- ❒ Conflict between project objectives and regular functions
- ❒ Overlap in project responsibilities, for example, conduct of similar quality control projects by different departments
- ❒ Potential for unreceptive attitude toward the project by the participating departments
- ❒ Multiple layers of management between the project personnel and the beneficiaries of the project
- ❒ ☹ack of concentrated effort (divided attention between project tasks and regular tasks)

Product Organization

Another approach to organizing a project is to use the end product or goal of the project as the determining factor for the organization structure. This is often referred to as the product organization. The project is set up as a unique entity within the parent organization. It has its own dedicated technical staff and administration. It is linked to the rest of the organization through progress reports, organizational policies, procedures, and funding. The interface between product organized projects and other elements of the organization may be strict or liberal depending on the organization. Product organization is common in large project-driven organizations. Unlike the other organization structures, product organization decentralizes functions. It creates a group consisting of specialized skills around a given task. The project group is sometimes referred to as a team or a task force. Product organization is also common in public and research organizations where specially organized and designated groups are assigned specific functions. A major advantage of product organization is that it gives the project members a feeling of dedication to and identification with a particular project goal. A possible shortcoming is the requirement that the project group be sufficiently funded to be able to operate independently without sharing resources or personnel with other functional groups or programs. At the conclusion of a project, the project team may be reassigned to other projects. Product organization can facilitate the most diverse and flexible grouping of project participants and permits highly dedicated attention to the project at hand. The advantages of product organization are:

- Full control by the project manager
- Direct responsibility of the project members to the project manager (one boss)
- Condensation of communication lines
- Skill development due to project specialization
- Improved motivation, commitment, and concentration
- Quicker decisions due to centralized authority
- Improved morale resulting from belonging to a given project
- Simplicity of structure
- Unity of project purpose

The disadvantages of product organization are:

- Duplication of effort on different but similar projects
- Monopoly of organizational resources
- Mutually exclusive allocation of resources (one person to one project)
- Narrow view of project personnel (as opposed to global organization view)
- Reduced skill diversification

- Concern about new job assignment after the project
- Need for a consistent source of project funding

Matrix Organization

Matrix organization represents a mixture of project organization and functional organization. It permits both vertical and horizontal flows of information. The matrix model is sometimes called a multiple-boss organization. It is a model that is becoming increasingly popular as the need for resource sharing increases. Engineering projects, for example, require the integration of specialized skills from different functional areas. Under matrix organization, projects are permitted to share physical resources as well as managerial assets. A matrix organization is suitable where there is multiple managerial accountability and responsibility for a job function. There are usually two chains of command, horizontal and vertical, dealing with functional and project lines. The project line in the matrix is usually of a temporary nature, while the functional line is more permanent. The matrix organization is quite dynamic, with its actual structure being determined by the prevailing project scenarios. The matrix organization has several advantages and some disadvantages. The advantages are:

Consolidation of objectives: The objectives of the task at hand are jointly shared and pursued by multiple departments.

Efficient utilization of resources: The allocation of company resources is more streamlined. Manpower and equipment can be allocated at the most suitable usage level jointly among departments working toward a common goal.

Free flow of information: Since departments are cooperating rather than competing, there is an unhindered flow of common information both vertically and horizontally in the matrix structure.

Interpersonal contacts: The joint responsibility for projects creates an atmosphere of functional compatibility. Good working relationships that develop under one matrix structure become useful in other projects.

High morale: The success achieved on one project effort motivates workers to cooperate on other projects.

Lateral functional interactions: The multiple responsibility for projects allows workers to be exposed to other functional activities and, thereby, permits smooth transition to other departments should that become necessary.

Post-project interactions: The matrix structure allows continuity of functions after project conclusion. The functional departments simply redirect their efforts to other responsibilities. Unlike a project organization structure, where project shutdown could necessitate layoffs, the matrix structure makes a provision for returning to regular responsibilities.

The disadvantages of the matrix organization are:

Multiple bosses: A major disadvantage of the matrix structure is the fact that workers report to two bosses on a given project. Playing one boss against another is a potential problem in a matrix structure.

Power struggle: A power struggle between the bosses may adversely affect the performance of the project personnel.

Complexity of structure: The number of managers and personnel involved in a given project can easily be confusing. Difficulties can arise with respect to monitoring and controlling personnel activities. Other potential problems are obstruction of information, slow response time, difficulty in resolving conflicts, unclear channels for supervision, and incompatibility of policies and procedures.

Overhead cost: By doubling up the chain of command, the matrix structure leads to higher interdepartmental and intradepartmental overhead costs. However, as productivity gains are realized, the overhead costs may become negligible.

Conflicting priorities: Since multiple responsibilities is a major characteristic of a matrix organization, it is sometimes difficult to determine which responsibility has higher priority. Each functional manager may view his own direct responsibilities as having higher priority than other project responsibilities.

Despite its disadvantages, the matrix organization is widely used. Its numerous advantages tend to outweigh the disadvantages. Besides, the disadvantages can be overcome with proper planning and coordination. This can be achieved through the Triple C model, discussed later in this chapter.

Mixed Organization

Another possibility for organizing a project is to adopt some combined implementation of functional, product, and matrix models. This permits a combination of the advantages of the various organization structures. The mixed model facilitates flexibility in meeting special problem situations. The structure can adapt to the prevailing needs of the project or the organization. However, a disadvantage is the difficulty in identifying lines of responsibility within a given project.

Selecting the Project Manager

A *project manager* is needed to direct the functional groups within the project organizational structure. The project manager has the overall responsibility for supervising the project planning, scheduling, and control functions. He or she must be very versatile with a broad range of knowledge covering analytical as well as managerial skills. The project manager must have both the power and authority to effectively pursue project goals within the confines of the prevailing project organizational structure. When selecting a project manager, several desirable characteristics and factors must be considered. These characteristics and factors include:

- Analytical and technical background
- Communication skills
- Leadership and managerial skills
- Availability, accessibility, and attentiveness
- Rapport with subordinates, peers, and top management
- Inquisitiveness

- ❒ Ability to be a motivator and a facilitator
- ❒ Familiarity with company operations
- ❒ Overall personality
- ❒ Perseverance
- ❒ Technical and administrative credibility

Work Breakdown Structure

Project decomposition and work simplification are important for enhancing project planning, scheduling, and control. A graphical tool for decomposing complex projects into a manageable structure is the work breakdown structure (WBS). A work breakdown structure is a hierarchical organization of the work elements contained in a project. Tasks that are contained in the WBS collectively describe the overall project. The WBS serves to describe the link between the end objective and the intermediate tasks. It shows work elements in a conceptual framework for planning, scheduling, and control. The objective of developing a WBS is to study the elemental components of a project in detail. It permits the implementation of the "divide and conquer" concepts. Overall project planning and control are substantially improved by using WBS. A large project may be broken down into smaller subprojects which may, in turn, be decomposed into task groups. Individual components in a WBS are referred to as WBS elements, and the hierarchy of each is designated by a level identifier. Elements at the same level of subdivision are said to be of the same WBS level. Descending levels provide increasingly detailed definition of project tasks. The complexity of a project and the degree of control desired will determine the number of levels in the WBS. The graphical structure of a WBS is similar to an organization chart, with different levels associated with different levels of detail about a project. The basic approach to developing a WBS is presented below:

- ❒ Level 1: Level 1 contains only the final project purpose.
- ❒ Level 2: Level 2 contains the major phases or subsections of the project. These phases are usually

identified by their contiguous location or by their related purpose.

- Level 3: Level 3 contains definable components of the level 2 phases.

Subsequent levels are constructed in more specific detail depending on the level of control desired. If a complete WBS is very large, separate WBS diagrams may be drawn for the level 2 components. A specification of work (SOW) or WBS summary should accompany the WBS. A statement of work is a narrative of the work to be done. It should include the objectives of the work, its nature, resource requirements, and tentative schedule. Each WBS element is assigned a code that is used for its identification throughout the project life cycle. Alphanumeric codes may be used to indicate element level as well as task group. The U.S. Department of Energy published a detailed guide for the preparation of a work breakdown structure. Interested readers should consult the reference for further details. The various management phases of a project can be condensed into three major functions of planning, scheduling, and control. In this book, various quantitative models are presented for project planning, scheduling, and control.

Project Planning

Project planning determines the nature of actions and responsibilities needed to achieve the project goal. It entails the development of alternate courses of action and the selection of the best action to achieve the objectives making up the goal. Planning determines what needs to be done, by whom, for whom, and when. Whether it is done for long-range (strategic) purposes or short-range (operational) purposes, planning should address the following components:

1. Project goal and objectives. This involves the specification of what must be accomplished at each stage of the project.
2. Technical and managerial approach. This involves the determination of the technical and managerial strategies to be employed in pursuing the project goal.

3. Resource availability. This requires the allocation of resources for carrying out the actions needed to achieve the project goal.
4. Project schedule. This involves a logical and time-based organization of the tasks and milestones contained in the project. The schedule is typically influenced by resource limitations.
5. Contingency plan and replanning. This involves the identification of auxiliary actions to be taken in case of unexpected developments in the project.
6. Project policy. This involves specifying the general guidelines for carrying out tasks within the project.
7. Project procedure. This involves specifying the detailed method for implementing a given policy relative to the tasks needed to achieve the project goal.
8. Performance standard. This involves the establishment of a minimum acceptable level of quality for the products of the project.
9. Tracking, reporting, and auditing. These involve keeping track of the project plans, evaluating tasks, and scrutinizing the records of the project.

Strategic Levels of Planning

Badiru outlined the strategic levels of planning. Decisions involving strategic planning lay the foundation for successful implementation of projects. Planning forms the basis for all actions. Strategic decisions may be divided into three strategy levels of *supra level planning, macro level planning,* and *micro level planning:*

Supra Level Planning: Planning at this level deals with the big picture of how the project fits the overall and long-range organizational goals. Questions faced at this level concern potential contributions of the project to the welfare of the organization, effect on the depletion of company resources, required interfaces with other projects within and outside the organization, risk exposure, management support for the project, concurrent projects, company culture, market share, shareholder expectations, and financial stability.

Macro Level Planning: Planning decisions at this level address the overall planning within the project boundary. The scope of the project and its operational interfaces should be addressed at this level. Questions faced at the macro level include goal definition, project scope, availability of qualified personnel, resource availability, project policies, communication interfaces, budget requirements, goal interactions, deadline, and conflict resolution strategies.

Micro Level Planning: This deals with detailed operational plans at the task levels of the project. Definite and explicit tactics for accomplishing specific project objectives are developed at the micro level. The concept of MBO (management by objective) may be particularly effective at this level. MBO permits each project member to plan his or own work at the micro level. Factors to be considered at the micro level of project decisions include scheduled time, training requirement, tools required, task procedures, reporting requirements, and quality requirements.

Project decisions at the three levels defined above will involve numerous personnel within the organization with various types and levels of expertise. In addition to the conventional roles of the project manager, specialized roles may be developed within the project scope. Such roles include the following:

1. **Technical specialist**: This person will have responsibility for addressing specific technical requirements of the project. In a large project, there will typically be several technical specialists working together to solve project problems.
2. **Operations integrator:** This person will be responsible for making sure that all operational components of the project interface correctly to satisfy project goals. This person should have good technical awareness and excellent interpersonal skills.
3. **Project specialist:** This person has specific expertise related to the specific goals and requirements of the project. Even though a technical specialist may also

serve as a project specialist, the two roles should be distinguished. A general electrical engineer may be a technical specialist on the electronic design components of a project. However, if the specific setting of the electronics project is in the medical field, then an electrical engineer with expertise in medical operations may be needed to serve as the project specialist.

Project organization is a crucial component of project planning. Organizing a project involves determining the interfaces needed among personnel in order to assure a dedicated pursuit of the project goal. It involves the determination of what activities should be performed in what functional areas and under what supervisory hierarchy. Staffing is a component of organizing. Staffing is the process of defining the required personnel and the assignment of the personnel to appropriate functions with respect to the project goal. The staffing process may include hiring new people, reassignment of existing personnel, training or retraining, and realignment of responsibilities. The Triple C model presented by Badiru is particularly useful for organizing a project. The model states that project management can be enhanced by implementing it within the integrated functions of:

- Communication
- Cooperation
- Coordination

The model facilitates a systematic approach to project planning, organizing, scheduling, and control. The Triple C principle is different from the 3C approach commonly used in the military. The military approach emphasizes personnel management in the hierarchy of command, control, and communication. This makes communication the last function. The Triple C, by contrast, suggests communication as the first and foremost function.

Communication

The communication function of project management involves making all those concerned aware of project requirements and progress. Those who will be affected by the project directly or indirectly, as participants or as recipients, should be informed as appropriate regarding the following:

- What is the project?
- Why is the project needed?
- Who is in charge of the project?
- What alternatives are available?
- What is the expected cost of the project?
- What penalties are associated with the project?
- Who will be affected by the failure of the project?
- What are the possible negative impacts of the project?
- What are the potential direct and indirect benefits?
- What precedents are available for the project?
- Who else already knows about the project?
- What personnel contribution is needed?
- When will the project be implemented?
- How will the project be organized?
- What is the project scope?

The communication channel must be kept open throughout the project life cycle. In addition to in-house communication, external sources should also be consulted as appropriate. The project manager must:

- Exude commitment to the project
- Develop a communication responsibility matrix
- Facilitate multi channel communication interfaces
- Identify internal and external communication needs
- Resolve organizational and communication hierarchies
- Endorse both formal and informal communication links

Cooperation

The cooperation of the project personnel must be explicitly elicited. Merely signing off on or giving a nod to a project is not enough assurance of full cooperation. The participants in and customers of the project must be convinced of the merits of the project. Some of the factors that influence cooperation in a project environment include manpower requirements, resource requirements, budget limitations, past experiences, conflicting priorities, and lack of uniform organizational support. A structured approach to seeking cooperation should clarify the following:

- The rewards of cooperation
- What cooperative efforts are needed
- The implications of lack of cooperation
- The criticality of cooperation to the project
- What time frame is involved for the project
- The organizational impact of cooperation
- The precedents for future projects

A documentation of the prevailing level of cooperation is useful for winning further support for a project. Clarification of project priorities will facilitate personnel cooperation. Relative priorities of multiple projects should be specified so that a project that is of high priority to the organization is also of high priority to all groups within the organization.

Coordination

After successfully initiating the communication and cooperation functions, the efforts of the project personnel must be coordinated. Coordination facilitates harmonious organization of project efforts. The development of a responsibility chart can be very helpful at this stage. A responsibility chart is a matrix consisting of columns of individual or functional departments and rows of required actions. Cells within the matrix are filled with relationship codes that indicate who is responsible for what. The responsibility chart helps to avoid neglecting crucial communication requirements and obligations. It can help resolve questions such as:

- Who is to do what?
- Who is to inform whom of what?
- Whose approval is needed for what?

- ❒ Who is responsible for which results?
- ❒ What personnel interfaces are involved?
- ❒ What support is needed from whom and when?

Management by Objective

Management by objective (MBO) is the management concept whereby the worker is allowed to take responsibility for the design and performance of a task under general guidelines. It is a planning tool that gives each worker a chance to set his own objectives in achieving project goals. The worker can monitor his own progress and take corrective actions when needed without explicit management intervention. Self-motivated workers seem to be best suited for the application of the MBO concept. The advantages of MBO include:

- ❒ It encourages the worker to find better ways of performing the assigned tasks.
- ❒ It avoids over-supervision of self-motivated workers.
- ❒ It raises the awareness of the worker about organizational goals and expectations.
- ❒ It permits timely feedback on worker performance.

However, MBO does have some disadvantages, which include possible abuse of the freedom to self-direct and possible disruption of overall project coordination.

Management by Exception

Management by exception (MBE) is an after-the-fact management approach to control. Contingency plans are not made and there is no strict monitoring of performance. Deviations from expectations are considered exceptions to the rule. When unacceptable deviations from plans occur, they are investigated, and only then is an action taken. The concept is also often referred to as management by crisis or crisis management. The irony of MBE is that managers that operate under crisis management are often recognized as superstars because they solve problems whenever they develop. On the other hand, managers that prevent problems may be viewed as inactive because they are rarely seen solving problems. The major advantage of MBE is that it lessens the management workload. However, it is a risky concept to follow. Management should work toward avoiding problems rather than exposing the organization to potentially expensive crisis management actions. A manager who operates under the notion of "if it is not broken, don't fix it" will never have the opportunity to improve the managerial process.

Project Scheduling

Project scheduling is a major function in project management. The project schedule shows the timing of the efforts and resources committed to the project. A master schedule for the overall project is often developed for general overview of a project. In addition, detailed work schedules are developed for specific segments or phases of the project. The detailed schedules serve as operating guides for the project personnel. Project scheduling should be distinguished from sequencing and scheduling in production management even though the same principles and procedures are applicable to both. Production sequencing involves ordering of operations on each machine (resource) so as to satisfy the sequence of operations required by a job. A sequence of operations on a job may require that the same type of operation be performed on the same job (or product) at different times while the job is in production. This may necessitate repeated routing of the job to the same machine (or resource center) at different times. Production scheduling provides a basis for determining when a job is routed from machine to machine for specific operations. This establishes the starting and finishing times of each operation. Production sequencing and scheduling involve developing relative priorities of operations at each machine in order to meet scheduled due dates of individual jobs. The method of prioritizing jobs is often referred to as the *dispatching rule* for sending jobs to resource centers. In production management, sequencing and scheduling are performed as complementary functions. By contrast, project scheduling deals strictly with the timing of tasks that must be performed in a project. This does not require a machine sequencing process. Even when a task requires multiple performance of the same action, each occurrence of the action is viewed as an activity that must be scheduled separately. Thus, project scheduling is a simplified form of the production scheduling problem. Project scheduling can be carried out as the specific means through which the tasks involved in production management are scheduled and accomplished. Project scheduling involves the following functions.

- **Time and Resource Estimation:** Estimates are made of the time and resources required to perform each of the network activities.
- **Basic Scheduling:** The basic scheduling computations are performed on a project network by using forward pass and backward pass computational procedures. These computations give the earliest and latest start and finish times for each activity. Schedule management often involves performing time-cost trade-off analysis. The scheduling procedure makes use of tools such as CPM (Critical Path Method), PERT (Program Evaluation and Review Technique), and Gantt charts.
- **Time-Cost Trade offs:** In this function, the time-cost trade-off analysis of activity performance times is conducted to determine the cost of reducing the project duration.
- **Resource Allocation:** Constrained resource allocation refers to the process of allocating limited resources to competing activities in a project. Scheduling heuristics or mathematical allocation models are used in allocating the limited resources during the scheduling phase. A database of resource availability should be developed for each project prior to starting the scheduling process.
- **Resource Loading and Leveling:** Resource loading develops the profile of the resource units allocated over time. Resource leveling refers to the process of shifting activities to reduce the period-to-period fluctuations in resource requirements.
- **Schedule Control:** When the network plan and schedule have been satisfactorily developed, they are

disseminated in final form for operational use. The schedule is tracked and controlled by comparing actual status to expected status at selected review times. Schedule tracking facilitates frequent review and revision of the project plan.

Project Control

Time, cost, and performance form the basis for the operating characteristics of a project. These factors help to determine the basis for project control. Project control is the process of reducing the deviation between actual performance and planned performance. Measurements are taken on each of the three project constraints of time, performance, and cost.

Performance may be expressed in terms of quality, productivity, or any other measure of interest. Cost may be expressed in terms of resource expenditure or budget requirements. Schedule is typically expressed in terms of the timing of activities and the expected project duration. It is impossible to achieve an optimal simultaneous satisfaction of all three project constraints. Consequently, it becomes necessary to compromise one constraint in favor of another. It presents a model of the trade-offs between performance, time, and resource (cost).

Better performance can be achieved if more time and resources are available for a project. If lower costs and tighter schedules are desired, then performance may have to be compromised and vice versa. From the point of view of the project manager, the project should be at the highest point along the performances axis. Of course, this represents an extreme case of getting something for nothing. From the point of view of the project personnel, the project should be at the point indicating highest performance, longest time, and most resources. This, of course, may be an unrealistic expectation since time and resources are typically in short supply. Thus, a feasible trade-off strategy must be developed. Even though the trade-off boundary is represented by a box, it is obvious that the surface of the box will not be flat. If a multifactor mathematical model is developed for the three factors the nature of the response surface will vary depending on the specific interactions of the factors for any given project.

If we consider only two of the three constraints at a time, we can better study their respective relationships. It shows some potential two-factor relationships. In plot (a), performance is modeled as the dependent variable, while cost is the independent variable. Performance increases as cost increases up to a point where performance levels off. If cost is allowed to continue to increase, performance eventually starts to drop. In plot (b), performance is modeled as being dependent on time. The more the time that is allowed for a project, the higher the expected performance up to a point where performance levels off. In plot (c), cost depends on time. As project duration increases, cost increases. The increases in cost may be composed of labor cost raw material cost and/or cost associated with decreasing productivity. Note that there may be a fixed cost associated with a project even when a time schedule is not in effect.

It shows an alternate time-cost trade-off relationship. In this case, the shorter the desired project duration, the higher the cost of the project. If more time is available for the project, then cost can be reduced. However, there is a limit to the possible reduction in cost. After some time, the cost function turns upward due to the increasing cost of keeping manpower and resources tied up on the project for a long period of time. The optimal duration of the project corresponds to the point where the lowest cost is realized.

Some of the causes of control problems in project scheduling, performance, and cost are summarized below:

Schedule Problems	***Performance Problems***	***Cost Problem***
Bad time estimates	Poor quality	High labor cost
Technical problems	Poor mobility	Inadequate budget
Change of due dates	Lack of training	Poor cost reporting
Precedence structure	Poor functionality	Effects of inflation

Schedule Problems	***Performance Problems***	***Cost Problem***
Unreliable time estimates	Maintenance problems	High overhead cost
Delay of critical activities	Lack of clear objectives	Increase in scope of work

Schedule Control

The Gantt charts developed in the scheduling phase of a project can serve as the yardstick for measuring project progress. Project status should be monitored frequently. A record should be maintained of the difference between the expected progress of an activity and its actual progress. This information should be conveyed to the appropriate personnel. The more milestones or control points there are in the project, the better the monitoring function. The larger number allows for more frequent and distinct avenues for monitoring the schedule. Thus, problems can be identified and controlled before they accumulate into a bigger problem. Some corrective actions that may be taken for schedule problems include:

- Crashing tasks
- Redesigning tasks
- Revising milestones
- Adjusting time estimates
- Changing the scope of work
- Combining related activities
- Introduction of new technology
- Eliminating unnecessary activities

Performance Control

Most project performance problems will not surface until after the project is completed. This makes performance control very difficult. However, every effort should be made to measure all the intermediate factors affecting the project. After-the-fact measurements generally do not facilitate good control. Some of the performance problems may be indicated by time and cost deviations. So, when schedule and cost problems exist, an analysis of how the problems may affect performance should be made. Since project performance requirements usually relate to the performance of the end products, controlling performance problems may necessitate the following:

1. Modifying policies and procedures
2. Introducing improved technology
3. Adjusting project specifications
4. Improving management control
5. Reviewing project priorities
6. Changing quality standards
7. Allocating more resources
8. Improving work ethics

Cost Control

Cost control has received extensive coverage in the literature. Numerous accounting and reporting systems have been developed over the years for project cost monitoring and control. Some of the strategies suitable for controlling project cost include:

- Reducing labor costs
- Using competitive bidding
- Modification of work process
- Adjusting work breakdown structure
- Improving coordination of project functions
- Improving cost estimation procedures
- Using less expensive raw materials
- Controlling inflationary trends
- Cutting overhead costs

The Triple C model presented earlier can be implemented for project control purposes. In The model shows the important interfaces between communication, cooperation, coordination, performance, cost, and schedule control.

Project Decision Model

Badiru presents decision steps for project management. The steps facilitate a proper consideration of the essential elements of decisions in a project environment. These essential elements include problem statement, information, performance measure, decision model, and an implementation of the decision. The steps recommended by Badiru for project decisions are outlined below.

Step 1. Problem Statement

A problem involves choosing between competing, and probably conflicting, alternatives. The components of problem solving in project management include:

- Describing the problem
- Defining a model to represent the problem
- Solving the model
- Testing the solution
- Implementing and maintaining the solution

Problem definition is very crucial. In many cases, *symptoms* of a problem are recognized more readily than its *cause* and *location*. Even after the problem is accurately identified and defined, a benefit/cost analysis may be needed to determine if the cost of solving the problem is justified.

Step 2. Data and Information Requirements

Information is the driving force for the project decision process. Information clarifies the relative states of past, present, and future events. The collection, storage, retrieval, organization, and processing of raw data are important components for generating information. Without data, there can be no information. Without good information, there cannot be a valid decision. The essential requirements for generating information are:

- Ensure that an effective data collection procedure is followed.
- Determine the type and the appropriate amount of data to collect.
- Evaluate the data collected with respect to information potential.
- Evaluate the cost of collecting the required data.

For example: Suppose a manager is presented with a recorded fact that says, "*sales for the last quarter are 10,000 units.*" This constitutes ordinary data. There are many ways of using this data to make a decision depending on the manager's value system. An analyst, however, can ensure the proper use of the data by transforming it into information, such as, "*sales of 10,000 units for last quarter are low.*" This type of information is more useful to the manager for decision making.

Step 3. Performance Measure

A performance measure for the competing alternatives should be specified. The decision maker assigns a perceived worth or value to the available alternatives. Setting a measure of performance is crucial to the process of defining and selecting alternatives.

Step 4. Decision Model

A decision model provides the basis for the analysis and synthesis of information, and is the mechanism by which competing alternatives are compared. To be effective, a decision model must be based on a systematic and logical framework for guiding project decisions. A decision model can be a verbal, graphical, or mathematical representation of the ideas in the decision-making process. A project decision model should have the following characteristics:

- Simplified representation of the actual situation
- Explanation and prediction of the actual situation
- Validity and appropriateness
- Applicability to similar problems

The formulation of a decision model involves three essential components: Abstraction: Determining the relevant factors Construction: Combining the factors into a logical model Validation: Assuring that the model adequately represents the problem

The basic types of decision models for project management are:

Descriptive models: These are directed at describing a decision scenario and identifying the associated problem. For example, a project analyst might use a CPM network model to identify bottleneck tasks in a project.

Prescriptive models: These furnish procedural guidelines for implementing actions. The Triple C approach, for example, is a model that prescribes the procedures for achieving communication, cooperation, and coordination in a project environment.

Predictive models: These models are used to predict future events in a problem environment. They are typically based on historical data about the problem situation. For example, a regression model based on past data may be used to predict future productivity gains associated with expected levels of resource allocation.

Satisfying models: These are models that provide trade-off strategies for achieving a satisfactory solution to a problem within given constraints. Goal programming and other multi-criteria techniques provide good satisfying solutions. For example, these models are helpful in cases where time limitation, resource shortage, and performance requirements constrain the implementation of a project.

Optimizing models: These models are designed to find the best available solution to a problem subject to a certain set of constraints. For example, a linear programming model can be used to determine the optimum product mix in a production environment.

In many situations, two or more of the above models may be involved in the solution of a problem. For example, a descriptive model might provide insights into the nature of the problem; an optimization model might provide the optimal set of actions to take in solving the problem; a satisfying model might temper the optimal solution with reality; a prescriptive model might suggest the procedures for implementing the selected solution; and a predictive model might predict the expected outcome of implementing the solution.

Step 5. Making the Decision

Using the available data, information, and the decision model, the decision maker will determine the real-world actions that are needed to solve the stated problem. A sensitivity analysis may be useful for determining what changes in parameter values might cause a change in the decision.

Step 6. Implementing the Decision

A decision represents the selection of an alternative that satisfies the objective stated in the problem statement. A good decision is useless until it is implemented.

An important aspect of a decision is to specify how it is to be implemented. Selling the decision and the project to management requires a well-organized persuasive presentation. The way a decision is presented can directly influence whether or not it is adopted. The presentation of a decision should include at least the following: an executive summary, technical aspects of the decision, managerial aspects of the decision, resources required to implement the decision, cost of the decision, and the time frame for implementing the decision.

Project Implementation Model

It is helpful to have a model that can be adopted for project implementation purposes. Presented below is a comprehensive model for the essential tasks in project planning, scheduling, and control.

1: Planning

I. Specify Project Background

A. Define Current Situation and Process

1. Understand the Process

2. Identify Important Variables

3. Quantify Variables

B. Identify Areas for Improvement

1. List and Explain the Areas

2. Study Potential Strategy for Solution

II. Define Unique Terminologies Relevant to the Project

1. Industry-specific Terminologies

2. Company-specific Terminologies

3. Project-specific Terminologies

III. Define Project Goal and Objectives

A. Write Mission Statement

B. Solicit Inputs and Ideas from Personnel

IV. Establish Performance Standards

A. Schedule
B. Performance
C. Cost
V. Conduct Formal Project Feasibility Study
A. Determine Impact on Cost
B. Determine on Organization
C. Determine Project Deliverables
VI. Secure Management Support

2: Organizing

I. Identify Project Management Team
A. Specify Project Organization Structure
1. Matrix Structure
2. Formal and Informal Structures
3. Justify Structure
B. Specify Departments Involved and Key Personnel
1. Purchasing
2. Materials Management
3. Engineering, Design, Manufacturing, etc.
C. Define Project Management Responsibilities
1. Select Project Manager
2. Write Project Charter
3. Establish Project Policies and Procedures
II. Implement Triple C Model
A. *Communication*
1. Determine Communication Interfaces
2. Develop Communication Matrix
B. *Cooperation*
1. Outline Cooperation Requirements
C. *Coordination*
1. Develop Work Breakdown Structure
2. Assign Task Responsibilities
3. Develop Responsibility Chart

3: Scheduling and Resource Allocation

I. Develop Master Schedule
A. Estimate Task Duration

B. Identify Task Precedence Requirements

1. Technical Precedence

2. Resource-imposed Precedence

3. Procedural Precedence

C. Use Analytical Models

1. CPM

2. PERT

3. Gantt Chart

4. Optimization Models

4: Tracking, Reporting, and Control

I. Establish Guidelines for Tracking, Reporting, and Control

A. Define Data Requirements

1. Data Categories

2. Data Characterization

3. Measurement Scales

B. Develop Data Documentation

1. Data Update Requirements

2. Data Quality Control

3. Establish Data Security Measures

II. Categorize Control Points

A. Schedule Audit

1. Activity Network and Gantt Charts

2. Milestones

3. Delivery Schedule

B. Performance Audit

1. Employee Performance

2. Product Quality

C. Cost Audit

1. Cost Containment Measures

2. Percent Completion versus Budget Depletion

III. Identify Implementation Process

IV. Phase out the Project

A. Performance Review

B. Strategy for Follow-up Projects

C. Personnel Retention and Releases

V. Document Project and Submit Final Report

The model above gives a general guideline for project planning, scheduling, and control. The skeleton of the model can be adapted for implementation as required for specific projects. Not all projects will be amenable to all the contents of the model. Customization will always be necessary when implementing the model.

Selling the Project Plan

The project plan must be sold throughout the organization. Different levels of detail will be needed when presenting the project to various groups in the organization. The higher the level of management, the lower the level of detail. Top management will be more interested in the global aspects of the project. For example, when presenting the project to management, it is necessary to specify how the overall organization will be affected by the project. When presenting the project to the supervisory level staff, the most important aspect of the project will be the operational level of detail. At the worker or operator level, the individual will be more concerned about how his or her job will be affected by the project. The project manager or analyst must be able to accommodate these various levels of detail when presenting the plan to both participants in and customers of the project. Regardless of the group being addressed, the project presentation should cover the essential elements below at the appropriate levels of detail:

- Introduction
- Project Description
- Goals and Objectives
- Expected Outcome
- Performance Measure
- Conclusion

Importance of Quantitative Project Analysis

The tools for project management can be classified into three major categories as outlined by Badiru:

1. Qualitative Models
2. Computer Models
3. Quantitative Models

While numerous books exist on the qualitative aspects of managing projects, very few books focus on the quantitative tools for project management. It is no longer effective to manage projects on the basis of technical expertise or managerial skills alone. Various skills and tools must be integrated for more effective project planning, scheduling, and control. Numerous publications treat qualitative project management. For example, Meredith and Mantel present a managerial approach to project management. Computerized project management has also received extensive coverage in the literature.

Several publications on quantitative models are available for general management applications. Examples are: Buffa and Dyer, Dallenback and George, Eck, Gordon and Pressman, Johnson and Winn, Kim, Lapin, Levin and Kirkpatrick, D. Smith, Thierauf, and Verma and Gross. But, very few books have been published specifically on the quantitative tools for project management.

Quantitative tools are just as important as other tools for project planning, scheduling, and control. In practice, it is essential to have a balanced mix of qualitative, computer, and quantitative tools in project analysis. Many of the components of the life cycle of a project can benefit from quantitative analysis. Although the scheduling and resource allocation functions are the most suitable for the application of quantitative models, the broad spectrum of project planning, scheduling, and control should be considered for the application of the quantitative models. This chapter has presented an overview of the various functions involved in project planning, scheduling, and control. The managerial aspects of project management were discussed briefly.

2

Need for Project Management

Introduction

Solutions for the staggering problems facing the world today have called for the development of ever larger and more complex systems. It is debatable whether project management (or systems management) was developed as a result of management's need for a technique to handle such complex problems. However, like the chicken and the egg, it is a useless argument. What is not debatable is the fact that today's big, complex problems require integrated, multidisciplinary efforts. Project management provides just such an approach to problems.

Recognizing the Need

In establishing the need for project management, there are some basic premises that must be recognized. First, every organization, whether public or private, produces a product, or provides a service, or does both. All of these organizations *want* to perform so that their goods or services are provided at the right time, at minimum cost (maximum profit), and to the satisfaction of the customer, client, or consumer. Evidence of lack of success in meeting these goals is found in business failures, firing or replacement of top executives, reduced profits, and rapidly expanding government bureaucracies. Sometimes the reasons for these failures are external, but more often than not, the fault is within the organization itself.

A major factor influencing the need for project management is the size of the organization. A very small organizational entity such as a consulting firm, engineering office, or even a small contractor who has a budget, a schedule, and limited requirements to control quality and production, probably could get along very well without using formal project management techniques. By virtue of its smallness, the few people involved can communicate rapidly and efficiently. Often, the same person is responsible for several interdisciplinary actions. The planner becomes the implementer (designer), scheduler, monitor, procurer, and director of construction on a simple noncomplex project. A whole hierarchy of organizations having projects of varying complexity can be listed, and at some point in this listing the need for project management becomes more and more evident. In an electric utility (a large organization) in which one department has a project involving one or maybe two disciplines, there really is no need for formal project management as previously defined. There is a clear point of responsibility (to whom the assignment was given). This individual (engineer) can be held responsible for control over the immediate subordinates (draftsmen, designer, typist, junior engineer, etc.). Actually, this person is the project manager, project engineer, and lead-discipline engineer for the work. In contrast, the same utility that is responsible for the design of a large complex nuclear-generating project involving a score of departments and many disciplines, will require project management in its most formal sense. Management found that they needed a formalized method to manage complex one-of-a-kind jobs. Size was not the key factor in the need for project management, rather it was organizational and project complexity.

Complex Projects

What happens when an organization is faced with accomplishing a very complex, multidisciplinary project? For instance, the Atlas missile program provides an early example of the use of project management in the aerospace industry. Up to this time the aerospace companies had attacked their problems within their hierarchical management organizations. They would set up task forces, giving functional managers responsibility for certain portions of the project, but with top management retaining overall responsibility. It worked, but with considerable difficulty, and with more or less constant organizational conflict.

Pure projects (fully projectized), such as the Manhattan project (or even the construction of the pyramids), where everyone on the project worked directly for the project manager, existed long before the Atlas program. However, the Atlas program has been said to be the beginning of modern project management, in that it was the first successful use of matrix management in an immensely complex "crash" program. The Atlas program was started in 1954 under Air Force Brig. Gen. Bernard A. Schreiver to develop the free world's first ICBM. "Because the Atlas program had started late and faced early and critical deadlines, the Air Force had to scrap accepted management principles and develop its own." Many management innovations were initiated, including: (1) direct program control by the Air Force and by a Special Projects Office, (2) the creation of the Ramo-Wooldridge Corporation to give overall technical advice to the program, (3) a speed-up of the development cycle by the use of "concurrency" by which major decisions were frozen early in the program and work on many different components went ahead simultaneously, and (4) the establishment (with Air Force insistence) of project offices by each contractor on the program.

As a result of the success of this and other government-sponsored programs, project management is now regarded as an essential part of all major systems acquisitions. Defense systems contractors rapidly recognized that project management had many advantages, and they established "mirror-image" organizations to their government customer. The defense contractors went one step further and developed what is now known as the matrix organization. The matrix has expanded the applicability of project management to the point where it can be successfully utilized by a wide variety of organizations.

Needs of Project Management

Project management has a very wide range of applicability; its present use only scratches the surface. It is equally useful in small or large organizations, and for small or large rich projects. Small projects can also benefit from the concentrated attention of a project manager with the attendant advantages of better budgetary and schedule control and better allocation of resources.

The principles of project management are applicable to every organization dealirg with complexity. In the past, project management has been widely used in the defense department, the aerospace industry, and in major construction projects. Now project management is gaining acceptance in product development, public works, nonprofit organizations, financial institutions, and in all sectors of government. It is particularly useful whenever considerable coordination is required between government agencies, between a government agency and a customer, or between a contractor and a client.

Organizational Considerations

In today's world of rapidly expanding technology and expanding influence and control by federal, state, and local government, organizations find it increasingly difficult to meet the complexities of a rapidly changing business environment. Most industrial, public service, and government organizations have met the problems of complexity by utilizing the hierarchical management structure inherited from the military. Top management has been very comfortable with the hierarchy because of its simple one-boss reporting system. The hierarchy also lends itself to convenient subdivision of an organization into groups or departments, each of which represents a specialty, discipline, or function. What could be more natural than to subdivide an organization into the same specialized disciplines that serve as departments in the university system? Staffing is simplified and specialists relate best to other specialists in their same discipline. These so-called line, functional, or disciplinary divisions often enhance efficiency and maximize productivity, but they also have some of the following inherent problems:

1. The ability of specialized organizational groups (line or functional divisions) to work together and to coordinate effectively with government regulatory agencies and/or clients is critical to the success of the organization. Line managers often suffer from "tunnel vision" in that they either don't know or don't subscribe to overall organizational goals. Often what's good for the division as perceived by the division manager may take precedence over what's best for the project or the entire organization.
2. Competition or feuding between line divisions may result in efficiency or failure to communicate vital information.
3. The responsibility for important external coordination may become muddled because of overlapping or inadequately defined responsibilities.
4. The division of responsibility for a job that overlaps several line or functional divisions (a project) usually slows and complicates the process of making decisions that affect the entire project. This may increase the possibility of inadequate or tardy response to changing conditions which could make the difference between project success or failure.
5. As organizations grow in size and organizational complexity, it becomes increasingly difficult for top management to concern themselves with the day-to-day problems of individual projects.

A chief executive may become faced with project failure and, in attempting to determine the cause for the failure, may find the division managers pointing the finger of blame at each other. Precious little objective information may be found as to what really went wrong.

Is Project Management Really Needed?

It can be a very traumatic experience for top management to realize that they really don't know what is going on. A chief executive in this position, faced with the problem of poor project performance, usually comes to the conclusion that a single point of information and control is needed if complex projects are going to be successfully conducted. Among the alternatives which can be considered is formalized project management. However, as previously indicated, project management is not for everyone, and should be used only if the situation demands it. In determining the need for project management, one should examine the project and the organization carefully and ask the following types of questions:

1. Is the job very large?
2. Is the job technically very complex?
3. Is the job a true system in that it has many separate parts or subsystems which must be integrated to complete the operational whole?
4. Is the job a part of a larger system and must it be closely integrated, particularly if the larger system has a project-oriented organization?
5. Does top management strongly feel the necessity of having a single point of information and responsibility for a total job?
6. Are strong budgetary and fiscal controls required?
7. Are tight schedule and budgetary constraints foreseen?
8. Are quick responses to changing conditions necessary?
9. Does the job cross many disciplinary as well as organizational boundaries?
10. Will the proposed job drastically disrupt the present organizational structure?
11. Are more than two divisions involved, and is more than one division going to be dealing directly with the client or customer?

12. Are there other complex projects being conducted concurrently with this one?
13. Is there likely to be conflict between line managers concerning this project?
14. Is the organization committed to a firm completion date?
15. Is it likely that changing conditions may seriously affect the project before its completion?
16. Are there major buys and procurements that must be made outside the company?
17. Are there major portions of the system which must be subcontracted outside the organization?
18. Is it necessary to have the project reviewed or approved by government regulatory agencies? Will these review processes and approvals be likely to generate problems and controversy?

If the answer to many of these questions is "yes," or even if there are only several "yes" answers concerning a phase of the project that is particularly critical, then project management should be seriously considered.

Alternatives to Project Management

The decision to introduce project management is a difficult one because it will require top management to give up some of its prerogatives, and line management to be partially or wholly subordinated to project management. It is an even more traumatic situation if the decision is to introduce a matrix organization, which is sure to be resisted by many old line, conservative managers. As previously indicated, project management is not for everyone, and it should only be used if it is really needed. There are four alternative methods of reorganizing which provide some of the benefits of project management. One of these alternatives should certainly be considered if top management does not want to relinquish authority, or if they decide that their projects are not sufficiently complex for project management. The alternatives to project management are:

1. Establishment of a "lead" division or discipline with responsibility to coordinate and sometimes direct the activities of the other affected divisions. This may suffice for smaller projects or in small organizations, but for large complex projects, conflict between project goal and the vested interests of the "lead" technical division may result in more problems than it solves.
2. Direct control over the project by top management. This is fine if top management has enough time to get involved in day-to-day project problems. If there is not adequate time, then the project and/or the entire organization may suffer if this alternative is chosen.
3. Clear definition of responsibility and authority of each organizational entity involved in the project. Even the clearest instructions may be misinterpreted or misunderstood, especially if the project is a complex one. This alternative is satisfactory if everyone is willing to cooperate fully, but most of the time this method sounds much better in theory than in actual application.
4. Establishment of a project coordinator who can accomplish one of the principal duties of a project manager, i.e., keep top management informed. However, the project manager cannot be held responsible for a project since she or he does not have decision making power or authority for project direction.

Task of Project Management

Once top management has decided that they should consider the use of project management, they must review what it can do for them. Are the benefits worth the trauma of implementing something new and very upsetting to their organization? What do they gain by implementing project management? What are the benefits?

Probably the most singular benefit provided by project management and its philosophy is its concerted and organized planning and control function. This is provided through a consistent and constant point of leadership by the project manager. Project management will centralize responsibility for the following key items in one individual:

1. Budgeting cost control
2. Schedules
3. Resource allocation
4. Technical quality
5. Client, customer, or public relations.

Budgeting Cost Control

If a project has complete definition, it has budgetary responsibility and/or at least cost-control responsibility. With many groups or organizational entities within a corporate structure, all having some degree of cost impact on the project, cost control must be implemented. The control responsibility can be delegated to subgroups, *but converges at the project manager's office.* Traditionally, the greatest impact to a project's cost comes from engineering and from construction units.

Budgeting is a part of the planning function, and also serves as a control mechanism giving the basis from which actual performance can be compared, measured, explained, and corrected. Control accounts are identified and established, each having component accounts needed for optimum control. The budget should be viewed and used as a program for planned expenditures. When the budget is combined with a schedule it serves as a program of physical completion and provides a most important tool of project management.

Schedules

No cost control program is effective if not coupled with the definitive schedule showing distinct, measurable, identifiable milestones. In addition, the schedule should show the interrelationship of one group's planned achievements with the other groups', thus identifying key interfaces. The complexity of the project will set the detail of this schedule. A schedule, however, must be a living document, easily understood, *previously committed to by its participants*, and readily adjusted to reflect current project conditions.

Developing construction schedules is relatively easy; however, developing engineering or design schedules is more difficult and least understood. Other important aspects deal with interfaces and constraints. If all a project manager does is to think out each of the key steps of design and construction, then establish the rational and logical activity sequence, the significant progress milestones toward completing the planning of the project will have been achieved. This, at least, establishes a reference point from which to make changes, and a basis to keep the interfaces clearly defined.

Resource Allocation

In addition to money and time the most important project resources are materials (and equipment) and manpower. Each project requires that some orderly process be followed in the procurement of materials, equipment, and services if it is to succeed. Without that orderly organization it is highly probable that planned costs and/or schedules will not be met due to the delay of delivery of key items.

After it has been determined what needs to be procured for a project, sequence and lead time must be determined to meet required delivery dates for the construction schedule. A Material Procurement Forecast is an extremely important document to manage this resource. It can identify key steps in the procurement process from development of specifications, through the bid cycle, vender prints, ending with delivery dates for any level of detail in material and equipment desired. Of course, the Material Procurement Forecast must be close-coupled with the project schedule.

The other aspect of this resource category involves manpower. The engineering/design manpower and construction or production labor make up the bulk of this resource. For the most part, this is a scarce and costly resource that is in high demand. Manpower requirements must be planned for in advance, often having to make compromises and tradeoffs according to priorities established.

In a large electric utility having many projects of varying importance and a relatively fixed number of personnel, project priorities were set up, ranking each of the projects according to importance and cost risks. The infighting and competition for manpower becomes much more objective and orderly when project management is used.

Technical Quality

Once a quality control system has been designed and documented, a design review process is in order. This should bring together experts and second-level supervision to review as a committee a pre designated segment of work.

With respect to manufacture and construction, a good "hold and witness" control plan must be developed with each specification. During construction, specific documented tests and witnessed operations are imperative. Any plan should include both source inspection and on-site inspection. Documented evidence of tests is also mandatory. In the nuclear power field, the subject of inspection has a very high priority and is almost of equal importance to getting the job done.

Start-up and acceptance testing should be outlined well in advance. Methodology and special measuring devices must be adequate. Prequalification of bidders can alleviate many of the future problems before they materialize. Procedures for inspection of delivered materials and equipment and documented damage reports are a must.

Client Customer, or Public Relations

One of the most important aspects of the project manager's job is the responsibility, as a representative of top management, to maintain good client, customer, or public relations. Top management occasionally interfaces with the client or customer, but the project manager is the day-by-day contact, particularly at the working level. The project manager must recognize and carefully plan for this phase of activity. If the client or customer finds that the project manager must continually refer to some member of the project team whenever a question is asked, the client or customer can rightly assume that the project manager is acting more as coordinator than as a manager. The project manager will eventually become bypassed when the client or customer needs information. It is quite likely that top management will then find the project manager's usefulness has ended.

Public relations are not always of concern to the project manager, however if the project is sensitive to the public interest because of environmental, marketing, or safety factors, then the project manager is deeply involved. The fact that there is a public aspect to almost every project cannot be ignored.

Summary

Formalized project management is not the solution to every organization's problems. Small, simple projects do not need formalized project management, but it is needed for large, complex, and multidisciplinary problems. There are many criteria that can be used as tip-offs indicating whether project management is really needed. The most important criteria are project complexity and top management's need for a single point of information, responsibility, and control for each project. There are four viable alternatives to project management, including the establishment of a lead division, direct control by top management, very clear definitions of responsibility and authority, and a project coordinator. However, each alternative has problems of implementation, and sound better in theory than in actual application. The need for project management is most apparent in the project manager's planning and control function which centralizes responsibility for the following key items in one individual: (1) budgeting cost control; (2) schedules; (3) resource allocation; (4) technical quality; and (5) client, customer, or public relations.

3

IMPLEMENTATION OF THE PROJECT

Introduction

The suggestion to use project management may come from any level of management; it might be limited to a single department or it might involve participation by the whole company or organization. For instance, a research department could implement project management in its own organization without involving the rest of the company. The decision to implement project management and the process of selling it to the organization are totally in the hands of the research director. The research director has the choice of pure project or matrix organizational forms and can experiment with variations to determine what works best in her or his organizational climate.

If the project or projects are large and involve the entire company's organization, the problem becomes more difficult since many organizational boundaries must be crossed and "empires" invaded. It doesn't really matter at which management level the suggestion to adopt project management originated, if it involves the entire organization the suggestion must go first to top management for approval. Project management is often "discovered" by members of middle management who then enthusiastically recommend it to top management. They fail to understand why the concept is not greeted with equal enthusiasm by top management and other members of middle management. Selling the concept to top management and obtaining their active, unqualified, and enthusiastic support is absolutely necessary for successful implementation of project management.

Top Management Actions

The most important of the many actions that must be taken in implementing project management are those which must be taken by top management. The most significant of these actions are:

1. Completely selling the project management concept to the entire organization.
2. Choice of the type or form of project organization to be utilized.
3. Issuance of a project charter to completely delineate project vs. functional authority and responsibilities.
4. Choice of project manager.
5. Choice of the right functional managers to participate in the project and/or matrix organization.
6. Supplying adequate resources to the project organization such as finances, equipment, personnel, computer support, etc.
7. Continuing support to the project manager.

This list of actions is more or less in the order that the actions must be taken, and most of them must be taken prior to the actual implementation of the project.

Selling Project Management

The entire organization must be prepared for project management particularly functional or line management. It is not enough that top management and the project office are strong project management supporters. The concept must also be sold throughout the organization as a "way of life." Strong top management support can nullify the problem of a few foot-dragging managers, but for project management to be really successful it must have continuing support from all levels of management. It is too late to implement project management after the contract has been received, the selling should have begun long before. In fact, a project staff and a project manager should have been appointed long before the arrival of the contract or the job.

How does top management sell the project management concept to the organization? It is apparent that first the support of middle management is essential. A management directive, although necessary, is not enough. An educational process is needed. A management training program can be initiated, using in-house training personnel or perhaps bringing in a consultant to conduct the training sessions. However, this process is usually time consuming, and it is too easy for attendees to beg off or miss sessions due to pressing company duties. A more effective approach is to send the managers in rotation to a concentrated two- or three-day professional seminar on project management, completely away from their job location. Such seminars are numerous in the larger cities. Perhaps an even more effective approach is the management workshop, preferably held as far away from the job location as possible. The workshops can be two- or three-day concentrated sessions held in a conference room of a local restaurant or hotel.

Experience has shown, however, that the most effective approach is the weekend retreat workshop. These can be held at a nearby resort or out of-town hotel. More and more hotels are providing capabilities for this type of event. The managers and their families check into the hotel, and the family goes its own way while the managers are free to spend their entire day, including evenings, learning about project management. These sessions, often irreverently referred to as "charm school" or "brainwashing," allow a concentrated dose of project management to be administered without interference from work. Top management should be present, not as instructors, but as participants in the discussions, and to demonstrate to their management that the implementation of project management is a joint undertaking of all management and that it has their unqualified support. The principal advantage of weekend sessions is that all involved management can participate at one time rather than in rotation. Top management can lead the discussions or they can call upon a knowledgeable management consultant to be the conference leader. In either case, participation and presentations by outside experts should be an important part of the program. The most important aspect of the program, however, should be the discussions in which management as a group decides how best to implement project management in their own particular organizational climate. Top management must realize that complete acceptance of the project management concept will come only after considerable soul searching and study by the management team. One weekend session may prove to be insufficient, and two sessions separated by time for thought and for homework may be more effective.

Choice of Type of Project Organization

The choice of the particular type or form of project management that top management wishes to implement depends entirely on decisions that only top management can make. These decisions should have been made during the initial project planning process.

Issuance of a Project Charter

Top management must provide a clear charter to the project manager. The charter may be simply a memo from the president or chief executive officer, or it may be an elaborate working document. In any case, a project organization charter should state "the purpose and meaning of organizational activities and ultimately direct the loyalties within and the stability of the structure." At the very least, the charter must spell out the responsibilities and authority of both project and functional managers. In addition, it can indicate, as much as possible, the project manager's relationships with the various functional managers involved in the project. That is, the charter should designate the desired organizational form. The initiation period of a project is no time for organizational experimentation. Not that the Project Charter should be "etched in stone," rather it should be sufficiently flexible to allow for periodic revision or organizational tinkering as indicated by management experience as the project progresses.

It is readily apparent that the project manager should be given adequate authority to do the job he or she is expected to do. The amount of authority is the question that must be faced by top management. How much of their own authority do they want to delegate, and to what extent do they wish to limit the authority and responsibilities of functional management? Top management is understandably reluctant to relinquish any of their authority or take it away from experienced and loyal functional managers. Top management must recognize that when they create a project manager who is expected to be held accountable for the success or failure of the project, they must give that project manager adequate authority. The causes for many a "sick" project can be traced to top management who held back and did not release sufficient authority to do the job. The project manager, being forced to check out most decisions with top management, becomes powerless to prevent disaster, and will probably end up as a convenient scapegoat when the project fails.

Choosing the Project Manager

The next important action is that of choosing a project manager. Top management must ensure that the right project manager is chosen, and that the selection is early in the formation of the project. Preferably the project manager should be the first person chosen so that she or he may then organize the project team.

Unfortunately it usually does not happen this way. A project is initiated, either as a result of a customer request (the receipt of a government contract or a successful bid on a client's project) or a product need (a potential commercial product indicated by marketing research). Hopefully, at this time a project or product manager would be chosen and the project would get off to a fast and positive start. As previously indicated, this does not always happen. Therefore, the project blunders on until a project manager is selected, and only then does the project really get underway. It would be much better if the project manager was assigned at the conception of the idea for the project. As soon as a customer or client need is determined, a project manager should be assigned. In this manner a single point of top management and customer or client contact is established as early as possible, and the project will be ready to function at full speed when the project is initiated.

Choosing the Right Functional Managers

It is often just as important to choose the right functional managers to work with the project as it is to choose the right project manager. A functional manager who is not a "believer" in project management, or perceives it as a threat, will be a roadblock to project progress, particularly when functioning in a matrix organization. Therefore, the nonbelievers should not be utilized in a matrix organization. Top management must recognize the nonbelievers in their management team and use them only in the type of functional organizational situation in which they can operate comfortably and effectively.

Supplying Adequate Resources

A vital function of top management is to supply adequate resources to their project managers. These resources may take many forms, but most important are financial support, project staff, service group support, and realistic priorities.

A certain amount of financial support is usually needed by projects to supplement direct project costs. This support often takes the form of burden or overhead charges for costs that could not be charged directly to the project because of contract or client constraints. Such costs could occur for the following types of needs:

1. Trips for attending conferences with clients, subcontractors, etc.
2. Trips and other costs to attend conferences and seminars to keep up with the state-of-the-art in the project area.
3. Hiring of consultants to solve special project problems.

Closely related to financial support is the provision for adequate staff support for the project office. Many of the project manager's problems involve lack of sufficient time to do the job right. Having adequate staff will alleviate this problem. Quite often job classifications such as administrative assistants, analysts, and planners cannot be charged directly to the project. Similarly, secretaries, clerks, and typists normally charge to overhead. Another type of support effort not always charged to contract is that of service organizations within the company. The problem is not just that a service effort may not be fully chargeable to a project, but that the service effort be of high quality and adequate to meet project needs. The following types of service-oriented functions must be provided to assure project success:

1. Editorial and printing support to prepare progress and other reports
2. Photographic support for test data and for report illustrations
3. Accounting support to provide timely reporting of project status
4. Computer service support to provide special programming expertise
5. Experimental machine shop and model shop support
6. Research and analytical laboratory support
7. Material and processes control laboratory support
8. Testing laboratory support
9. Purchasing support.

In addition, such organizations as quality control, logistics, value engineering, reliability, configuration management, and safety may or may not be part of the main stream of the project effort, but certainly have to be available and adequate for project needs.

Adequate service is dependent not only on the existence of adequate supporting organizations, but on the priority given the project in these organizations. Top management has the responsibility of ensuring that the relative priorities between projects and between project and functional organizations are realistic. Priorities are not only important for service support, but also for the use of materials and equipment, both company and government owned. Priorities must be adequate to ensure that materials and equipment can be purchased on schedule according to the Project Material Procurement Forecast and the Project Plan. Priorities should also ensure that the best qualified available personnel will be assigned to the project. Project priorities must guide the tradeoffs in materials, equipment, and personnel that must be made to determine which project gets what resources.

Continuing Top Management Support

Top management cannot simply implement project management by giving it their blessing and then forget about it. Continuing support is necessary and applies to all of the resources previously mentioned. Project needs and priorities should be continuously or frequently reviewed by top management to assure that the project remains healthy.

Functional Management

Functional management in a matrix organization must also take an important action. The attainment of project goals and objectives can be endangered by inaction or "foot-dragging" on the part of functional management and personnel serving on the project team. Therefore, functional management must not only accept the concept of project management, but they must obtain complete support from their organizational personnel.

Actions by The Project Manager

Now that the top management has successfully implemented project management and has given it full support, the action passes to the newly appointed project manager. There are a number of specific actions that must be initiated by the project manager to start the project on the road to success. The most critical of these actions are:

1. Issuance of the Project Implementation Plan

2. Creation of the Project Work Breakdown Structure (WBS)
3. Development of the project organization
4. Issuance of the Project Procedures Guide
5. Implementation of reporting and review procedures
6. Issuance of the Project Material Procurement Forecast
7. Issuance of Work Authorizations.

These actions are more or less sequential, although they are strongly interrelated and must be worked on at the same time. The most important consideration is that documentation implementing these actions be issued as early in the project life cycle as possible. Hopefully, much of this effort will be accomplished prior to the initiation of the project, such as during proposal preparation. Even so, a great deal of effort is required during the "front end" of a project to accomplish these actions.

Issuance of the Project Implementation Plan

The project manager, recognizing the responsibility of taking the first step toward getting the project going, puts together an initial project document usually called the Project Implementation Plan. This is the first step in developing an overall project plan, which will come a little later in the project. The implementation plan is necessary in either a pure project or a matrix organization, but is absolutely unavoidable in a matrix where there are many functional managers who must be informed about the following types of project information:

1. What must be accomplished?
2. What are the specific goals and objective?
3. What are the important constraints in terms of the schedule and budgets?
4. What specific organizational units will be involved in the project?
5. What are the important milestones in the project?
6. What are the important interface events in the project where hardware, facility, or other completions must be integrated?

7. What detailed planning must the project organizational units accomplish in support of the project and how early in the project?
8. How does the actual contract differ from the proposed work statement?

In the Project Implementation Plan the first cut must be made at breaking the project down into manageable pieces or work packages, usually only major subsystems at this point. The project should also be broken down into a rough time schedule for the completion of each subsystem or task, which will usually be presented as a simple bar chart. As can be seen, the major purpose of the Project Implementation Plan is to alert management as to the actual scope of the project and the role of their organizational unit in conducting the effort. Much of this effort will have been accomplished during the proposal stage. However the details must be covered in this official document which, in reality, serves to turn the project on and informs the project team what they must accomplish.

Creation of the Project Work Breakdown Structure

The project manager's next important task is to produce a detailed Work Breakdown Structure (WBS). The purpose of the WBS is to break the total project down into sufficiently small subdivisions to permit accurate cost estimates, and to permit adequate visibility and control. A second purpose of the WBS is to ensure that the smallest subdivisions represent tasks that can be readily accomplished within the estimated cost and schedule. Thus, the WBS is not only an important control tool, but it is extremely useful as a planning and estimating method. That is the reason for placing it in the position of the second project implementation action.

The development of a WBS is a contractual requirement for the acquisition of most defense material items, particularly research and development. In developing the WBS, the project office must work very closely with the functional and/or project subdivision managers who must actually perform the cost estimates and can best plan the work breakdown. An important goal is to keep the smallest work packages within single organizational units, if possible, in order to simplify cost and schedule estimating and control.

The technique of accomplishing the WBS consists of subdividing the project into major subdivisions (subsystems or subprojects), then to subdivide further into tasks, then into subtasks, and so on until the smallest practical unit (work package) is reached. The WBS is extremely important as it can tie all of the implementing and control actions of the project manager together. It can be the common framework for the Project Implementation Plan, for the project organization, and for the issuance of schedules, budgets, and work authorizations. This results in an integrated WBS, schedule, and budget.

Development of the Project Organization

Only good people can ensure project success. While this statement is true for any type of organization, the consequences resulting from inadequate personnel can be much more disastrous in a project since a relatively small slippage can mean project failure. In a pure project, the project manager has a free hand in developing his or her organization, and in selecting and/or hiring the project personnel. However, in a matrix the project manager can only select the project office personnel, and must negotiate with functional managers for the people who will do most of the work on the project.

How does the project manager know who are good people? In most cases, the functional manager's advice must be taken. But the project manager should always be on the lookout for people with the particular technical ability or managerial talent that is needed. In particular, project management and top management should always be watching for those people in the functional organizations who possess the unique qualities which can lead to their being successful project and assistant project managers. This talent is always in short supply, as discussed later in this chapter. In any case, the reservoir of people is in the functional organizations, and the project manager must negotiate with the functional managers for the services of the people she or he wants to work on the project.

A formal document should be issued by the project manager in which the project organization is outlined in detail and the status of everyone working on the project is clarified.

Project Procedures Guide

The fourth important implementing document that should be produced by the project office is the Project Procedures Guide. This document is designed to detail how the daily business of the project should be carried out, and it should contain the following types of procedures:

1. The duties and responsibilities of staff reporting to the project office
2. The duties and responsibilities of functional personnel working on the project
3. Time-keeping methods
4. Methods of obtaining priorities
5. Methods for resolving priority and conflict problems
6. Type and frequency of computer feedback of project expenditure and schedule status
7. The formal or contractual reporting and review procedures
8. The informal reporting and review procedures.

For the most part, these procedures need no further comment. The exception is the reporting and review procedures, which will be discussed in the next section.

Implementation of Reporting and Review Procedures

The project manager needs effective reporting and review procedures to effectively keep on top of activities and their status in the project. These procedures should be implemented early in the project and not allowed to be set aside whenever a crisis occurs. Reporting procedures must mesh with contractual requirements for customer reports and reviews, and will consist of formal reports, project review conferences, and informal contacts.

Formal Reports and Reviews

Formal reporting procedures are usually customer or client requirements and are out of the hands of the project office. However, the project manager usually needs to implement his or her own formal reporting procedures. All report inputs must go to the project office prior to being made a part of formal reports. The project manager must schedule regular project reviews as often as necessary.

These meetings should be scheduled well ahead of time, and the desired attendees should be informed of their responsibilities for presentations. Regular reporting of project status and of significant or interesting events in their area of responsibility should be reported. Special formal reviews should be scheduled if the project finds itself in a crisis.

Informal Reports and Reviews

Informal reports are equally important, but differ primarily in that they are not regularly scheduled and have no standard format. The project manager should be in close enough contact with the principal members of the project team so that daily or more frequent informal reports are received. The project team should make sure that the project manager is never placed in the position of being surprised. That is, the project manager should be the first to know of any problems, and always be on top of every aspect of the project. The project manager who, unaware of a potential problem, is called in for an informal briefing to top management will be extremely unhappy. Informal reviews will only be called if a special problem arises, and the project manager feels the necessity of obtaining immediate consultation with all concerned parties.

War Room

Most projects, regardless of size, require the use of a single, central conference room to hold design reviews, progress report meetings, and meetings with the customer or client. The project manager's office is usually too small for such meetings unless the project is very small. A general-use conference room, while adequate for holding meetings, is of no use as a tool for promoting good communications, project togetherness, and esprit de corps. It is a valuable asset to have a room that is solely used for the project. The project manager and personnel cannot only hold project meetings, but can also maintain briefing charts, data, models, and various project progress displays in this room. The room would be available to all members of the project team, and all levels of technical and administrative personnel would be encouraged to utilize it. Such rooms are variously referred to as the project room, the war room, or the project control room. It should be a comfortable room, of adequate size to hold the largest group desired, quiet, and with comfortable chairs. In addition to provisions for projecting and displaying data, it should have an abundance of blackboard space to encourage group discussions.

During the implementation stage of a project the war room can be of great help in creating a project team spirit. It serves as a symbol of the project to both top management and the customer. All members of the project team should become used to meeting regularly in the same place where they can communicate and solve problems together in familiar surroundings.

Project Material Procurement Forecast

In order to ensure an orderly and well-run project, a Project Material Procurement Forecast should be issued early in the project life cycle. The successful integration of most interfaces are dependent upon carefully scheduled procurements. This forecast is not only a necessary planning tool for alerting functional managers to the procurement schedule, but it also serves to highlight critical and long-lead time items. Such items as raw stock for fabrication may be overlooked without this forecast.

Issuance of Work Authorizations

The last of the implementing actions of the project manager is the issuance of work authorizations, although as a result of project urgency, this action often precedes some of the other actions previously discussed. The work authorization allocates project funds to the functional and/ or project organizational unit for the accomplishment of their portion of the effort. The work authorizations allocate funds to the individual work packages indicated in the WBS.

Job of the Project Manager

The project manager's job consists primarily of following good management practice. First and foremost, the project manager, like any manager, must be skilled at getting the job done through people. However, there are several key differences between the job of the project manager and that of general or functional/line management. The project manager must be very concerned with and skilled at carrying out the function of systems integration. As the single point of systems responsibility and authority, the project manager is the only person in the right spot to assure that integration takes place. Another characteristic of the job of project manager is to act as the center of a vital communications network linking together all parts of the project, including top management and the customer.

In addition, the project manager usually has very large, wide-ranging responsibilities much more extensive than equivalent level functional managers. The responsibilities sometimes appear to be overwhelming, yet there is not a commensurate high level of authority and salary. If the project is successful, the project manager seldom receives accolades or cash awards; she or he merely goes on to the next project. It only takes one unsuccessful project to cut a career short as a project manager, and the project manager runs the risk of being the scapegoat if the project fails. Project management is a high-pressure job, full of risk and uncertainty, and it is very often a thankless job.

It would seem that a prospective project manager should consider very carefully whether to accept the position. However, there are very real rewards in project management. Project management is where the action is, and where there are unlimited opportunities to excel. There is great satisfaction in having successfully completed a total project, a satisfaction seldom realized by functional management. In addition, project management's wide-ranging nature gives great freedom of action and wide opportunities for creative accomplishment. This has been very well supported by Charles Martin: "Projects daringly conceived and imaginatively executed offer great opportunities for talented people. Indeed, the freeing of creative people from inhibiting rules and bureaucratically restrictive environments can be the best reason for establishing a project. When a project achieves the delicate balance between bringing out the best of inventive thinking and providing adequate controls to ensure that efforts are directed toward project goals, then it is headed for a striking record of success." Thus, the rewards in project management are found in the personal satisfaction obtained from superior performance in a difficult job.

Selection of the Project Manager

Why should it be difficult to select a good project manager? Can't any competent, experienced manager do the job? If so, why do project managers usually seem to be in short supply? Recognizing promising candidates should be an easy matter if there are means of identifying the characteristics necessary for successful performance in project management. It is risky to attempt to list all of the personal characteristics necessary for success in project management. Since everyone has different management styles it is impossible to stereotype the proficient project manager. How then can prospective project managers be selected? There have been several attempts to suggest the type of person who would make the best project manager. These studies concluded that the project manager needs to have all the attributes of any middle-level good manager, but with particular strength in human relations skills. Therefore, the project manager should be strong in communicating, motivating, and team-building skills. The project manager must also be multidisciplinary oriented and innovative, possess integrative skills and have a high tolerance for rapid change and frustration.

The principal reservoir of project talent is in the line/functional organization, although project managers can be brought in from outside the organization. There are two approaches: (1) choose proven, successful line managers as project managers, and (2) develop a cadre of potential project managers by bringing promising candidates into the project office to gain experience as assistant project managers, planners, or other functions.

The first approach is the simplest in that mature, experienced managers of proven ability can be utilized. After the completion of the project, the manager can return to a line position if so desired. The alternative of having a line manager wear a second hat as a project manager is often utilized. Choosing the right manager can be a problem since success in a line/functional position does not necessarily guarantee success as a good project manager.

The second approach is more expensive, but it is more assured of success. A cadre of potential project managers is continuously maintained by viewing the project staff as trainees for the big job. Everyone brought into the project office is screened for his or her potential and continuously reviewed for suitability for project management. The problem involves first locating promising candidates, and then extricating them from their positions in the line/functional organization.

The potential project manager is faced with a career decision. One can remain in the line/functional organization and be assured of a relatively certain career path up the functional line of management, or one can enter the project office. For project management to be an attractive career path, it must have compensations and rewards. The rewards to be gained from personal satisfaction can be great and can be very important to the right person. For the generalist who is interested in the "big picture," project management is a very rewarding job, and it can be a career path leading to top management.

The challenge to top management is to identify individuals relatively early in their careers who have the basic attributes to become project managers. Project management is not for everyone. The men or women who like their jobs to be disciplined, orderly, unchanging, and conducted according to relatively fixed sets of rules, will not be comfortable in project management. This probably explains why functional managers often have difficulty making a transition to project management. Their management style was more suited to the ordered life typical of a specialist/functional organization. It is usually a traumatic experience to drastically change one's management style. In addition, the temporary nature of projects does not appeal to many people.

Change is the name of the game in project management. Project success is often dependent on rapid change. Prompt action by the project manager is necessary whenever a project runs into trouble. Delay usually only makes the problems worse. The project manager must be willing to change the rules, or break them if necessary, to get the job done.

The background of a project manager will usually include a degree in science, engineering, business, or whatever preparation necessary to understand the basic technology of "business." It is most important that the project manager be able to communicate with the technical specialists working on the project. Therefore, the project manager's educational background will be most likely to match the major technical needs of the project. Since most large projects have a very significant technical content, the project managers quite often are engineers. Engineers also often have the necessary total-system, multidisciplinary orientation.

Training of Prospective Project Managers

The identification of promising candidates for the position of project manager is just the first step. The next question is can project management skills be increased or developed? Such skills can be developed by either a training program, by experience, or both. Training programs are particularly useful to help the members of the project team who are working up the ladder. Such programs might consist of combinations of university courses, professional seminars or short courses, presentations by consultants, and in-house presentations by key project and top managers.

However, the real essence of the job of project manager can only be learned by experience. Therefore, the use of the project office as a training ground is very important. Prospective project managers can be given successively more responsible positions until they are fully prepared for the big job.

Summary

Project management can be implemented with a minimum of trauma and organizational conflict. If project management is to get started on the right foot, it depends upon top management, functional management, and project management making a number of critical actions very early in the life of the project. The most important action to be taken by top management is that of completely selling the project management concept to the entire organization. A number of other actions must be taken by top management which all involve firm and continuing support of the project manager and the project concept. The action then passes to functional and the newly appointed project manager.

Functional management must ensure that their organizations provide full support to the project manager. The project manager has seven very important actions, all of which involve ensuring that everyone on the project team knows what has to be done and when it has to be done.

4

Organising and Controlling for Project Management

Introduction

The most traumatic aspect of the process of implementing project management is the extensive reorganization or realigning of the existing organization that is necessary. However, it pays not to get too carried away in completely reorganizing; the more drastic the changes, the more the likelihood of failure. In addition, it must be remembered that the project management organization is an integral part of the existing management structure, and must be compatible with it. The form of project management must be chosen to fit the requirements of each particular organization and management structure. An organization does not completely start over with entirely new rules and new management. Most of the old rules and the old top management structure will still be there, and project management must be adapted to fit these organizational constraints.

Implementing project management need not change the original parent organization, but it may greatly alter it. A project organization will emerge emphasizing accomplishment of project objectives rather than optimizing the performance of functional departments. This is good because the project organization promotes the company viewpoint. Project management not only creates a new decision-making process, but complicates interpersonal relationships and new organizational interfaces. All these changes are complex and, to a degree, disruptive, but they are tolerated because of their contribution to overall effectiveness and efficiency.

This chapter presents some important organizational issues that need consideration before embarking on project management. The most critical facet of project management is the character of the project. There is a variety of project management "forms" which lead to the effective management of projects. The cause and effect of project objectives, information, and decision making are translated into organizational relationship roles called liaison personnel, expediters, coordinators, project administrators, project managers, project teams, and matrix management.

While these labels may be new to some organizations, the roles have usually been present in successful companies. In today's more complex and fast-moving business world, these relationship roles play a more significant part in achieving overall organizational goals by their sheer integrating force. Things get done because somebody is watching over the myriad of activities that traditionally overlap unyielding department boundaries. Things get *done better* because of the synergistic effect of team work.

This chapter concludes by directing these organizational issues into one focal point the project manager and ultimately proposes that results still depend on effective leadership of a *single* manager and her or his innate ability to influence the outcome of a project through the *active support* of other people.

With the existing state-of-the-art in project management should be considered only if the characteristics of a potential project require a change in the organization and the information systems of the company. Otherwise, the project can be assigned to a "can do" type department head and handled with the existing organization. The project definition model can be used as a basis for determining whether there is a compelling reason to use project management at all. At this point, a conscious decision must be made to supplement the organization and the information *before* implementation. This decision must come from top management with emphasis and clarity that project management is the direction in which the company is heading. Once the decision is made, a certain amount of fanfare is acceptable to set the stage, but top management must follow-up with active and visible support. Part of top management's decision process should include an assessment of the company's organizational climate with a corresponding directive as to the type of project organization to carry out the effort. Therefore, matching the project characteristics to the organization is an essential step in determining the extent and type of project management necessary. Project characteristics are:

1. Objective — expected results
2. Schedule — time span and when needed
3. Complexity — technological requirements
4. Size and nature of the task
5. Resources required — people and money
6. Organizational structure
7. Information and control systems.

All projects essentially follow this process. This Project Definition Model provides a clearer definition of the project, its impact on the organization, and the plan for its accomplishment.

Project Definition Model (PDM)

Since all projects have similar characteristics it is axiomatic that they follow a similar development and maturing process. This process is illustrated by the Project Definition Model (PDM). The PDM may be used as a framework for analysis and will result in a clear description of the project work, a plan for its accomplishment, and the impact of the project on the sponsoring company.

Every project is a manifestation of some management need or a desire to accomplish some specific task. It could be simply the design and programming of a computer system to control inventory, as complex as harnessing the sun to produce electric energy for commercial use, or even as remote as a research and development project to find a new drug for curing the common cold.

All projects start with some objectives and a schedule. The schedule at this early stage may be just a timeframe or a target date when results are desired. In any event, the first step in the PDM is to establish an objective and a schedule.

The next PDM step is a conceptual question that demands a definitive answer. Is the technology available to accomplish the objective and the schedule? Without the available technology it becomes necessary to go back and reconsider the purpose and necessity of the objective. Can an alternative be found which will achieve similar results? How important is the schedule? A brief survey of the computer state-of-the-art usually indicates that adequate technology is available for an inventory control system. However, in the case of harnessing the sun for producing electric energy, new technology must be developed. As a result, while it is still possible to desire the same objective, the schedule will have to be extended to accommodate the development of new technology. A good crystal ball or a soothsayer would be helpful at this point. If all else fails, a useful rule of thumb indicates that results from research and development efforts take approximately fifteen to twenty years to become commercially available. Except in rare R&D situations, a general approach would be to assume that the adequate technology is available and proceed to the next step, which is determining project strategy.

Determining project strategy means creating a step-by-step plan which will be used to meet the objective and schedule. Such a plan should include the sequence of these steps, how long each will take, and when the work will be done. The plan might also identify what kinds of skills and talents are needed to perform the project work. Upon completion of the project strategy, the next question concerns the availability of resources such as money, people, material, equipment and energy. If the company does not have enough systems analysts and programmers to design their computer system, perhaps there is enough money to purchase a ready-made system, or to contract for its programming and implementation. In the case of solar energy, while solar technology exists in controlled laboratory settings or in limited quantities, extensive production for commercial use will require considerably more applied scientific knowledge and funds. Many sponsors must be found to commit these vast resources before proceeding with the project work. Thus, it can be seen that executing project strategy relies heavily on having the available resources. The project strategy must match the available resources, but it also depends on the available technology. If resources are not sufficient, then it becomes necessary to return to the available technology question and start over. Before the project plan is ever developed, it is highly probable that in most of the complex programs the first steps of the PDM are iterative in nature. There must be a match between all constraints such as objective, schedule, technology, strategy, and resources, until a plan is finalized. Thus, the project plan depends on having a reasonable fixed objective and schedule with available technology and available resources.

According to accepted management practices, organizational *structure* follows operating *strategy*. In the PDM the project plan essentially represents the strategy of a project. How then should the organization be structured to accommodate the project plan? The foremost question becomes: Can the project be handled through the normal information and decision-making processes of the existing organization? If the present organization can support the project without change, a liaison leader can be assigned to execute the project plan. However, if the organization needs to be changed in order to handle the project work, a project team should be established. Running concurrently with this organizational question, there is also the question of systems. Are the control systems available for monitoring, reporting, analyzing, and controlling the progress of the project? Are there systems in place that can perform the functions of estimating, planning, scheduling, cost control, and resource allocation? Are these systems operational so that they can be used by the organization to control the project? If the answer is no, then control systems need to be developed to support either the existing or the new organization. The project team should be involved in the overall development and implementation of the control systems. It is unwise to execute the project plan until the project team has been established and the control systems are implemented.

The very existence of project management is contingent on two critical issues: (1) whether the organization needs changing, and (2) whether new control systems need to be developed, separate and apart from the existing systems of the sponsoring company. The degree of project success is directly proportional to the effectiveness of the information and decision-making processes. Efficient and effective management of projects demands strict attention and adherence to the PDM. However, in most cases, while all the steps are performed, they need not necessarily be completed in the order started.

The PDM can be used to determine project management needs because it brings to the surface the "hard" questions that need management attention. Ultimately, the right answers are furnished to get the job done.

Project

Consider an R&D project in the materials handling field. The customer, a large trucking company was looking for a method to transport small freight shipments cross-country with a minimum of handling. One solution was some form of containerization. But the size, shape, weight, and handling mechanisms required engineering design, tooling, operations, testing, etc. The technology was researched and found lacking except for some exotic containers used by the military in airlift operations. A project strategy was determined to design and build several prototypes for testing on high-volume freight routes. The project plan and schedule were developed to fabricate and test a dozen containers.

The project, assigned to a lead engineer, lasted six months and cost under $100,000. No organizational changes or new control systems were necessary for its execution. The result was a satisfactory design for freight containers which became the forerunner of today's modular truck container equipment. The container project may be considered an example of a small, uncomplicated project, requiring only a very limited project organization.

On the other hand, a project to build a nuclear-generating station costing approximately $1 billion with a ten-year schedule produces a different set of conditions. Although the same Project Definition Model is applicable, the complexity of the project, its magnitude, and the amount of resources required demands a different organization to direct the project effort separately and apart from the normal functional departments of the company.

Special information and control systems are needed to support the project team and to keep top management abreast of progress. While the following is not a comprehensive systems description, it illustrates the magnitude of the systems effort. Elaborate network cost and schedule systems with resource allocation capability are developed to handle upward of 20,000 engineering and construction activities at different levels of detail. Special computer programs are used to perform electric cable design and isometric interference studies (necessary to prevent pipes, cable, and equipment from literally running into each other during construction). Gigantic one-time inventory control systems are created to track and account for the approximately 100,000 material line items. Finally, detailed project information must be summarized into simple but meaningful progress reports for management. A full-time project manager, with decision-making authority, is necessary to lead the project team of selected experts from the functional departments. The nuclear project may be considered an example of a very large and complex project requiring very strong project management.

While these two examples differ widely in size and scope, the Project Definition Model still applies and illustrates the organizational flexibility available. The trucking firm's R&D containerization project is typical of the limited use of project management. Factory expansion projects or developing new products are borderline situations. It may be prudent to consider project management if the project is a one-time effort and the stretching of supervisory controls and inter department communications links appears risky. This is especially important since final results and existing information systems seldom meet the needs for urgent project decisions.

At the other end of the scale are very large and complex projects which have a compelling need for project management. However, as projects increase in size and duration, they eventually fall prey to the same bureaucratic system that their parent companies turned away from when they adopted project management. This occurs because the project is as large and complex as the parent organization without becoming a separate division or subsidiary company. In the planning are several large construction efforts where a single project, involving billions of dollars and spanning a dozen years, has a project organization which is almost a duplicate of its hierarchical parent company.

Admittedly, there are some ideas that never develop into projects. Use of the Project Definition Model will help to identify most of these situations. However, ideal use of the model assumes a fixed objective and schedule. This is not always practical. Sometimes original objectives never reach the strategy stage because technology is unavailable. In one case, a large company cancelled its Management Information Systems Project because the computer software technology was not available to meet its processing requirements. It had to settle for modified computer programs with manual support systems.

Changing Project Organization

The unique and complex character of projects creates considerable uncertainty in decision making and forces business organizations and their information systems into a different mold. This uncertainty is amplified by the sense of urgency inherent in project work. Considerable pressure is placed on the decision maker by time and schedule constraints.

As uncertainty increases, business organizations respond in two ways.

They either reduce the amount of information needed for project decisions, hoping for the best, or they increase their capacity to handle information through some other more costly means. Reducing the amount of information is unacceptable because it results in poor decisions, lowers performance, and increases the risk of project failure.

Project management fills the need to bring information closer to the decision maker. One step toward meeting this requirement is through development of formal information systems and procedures called Project Control Systems. Traditionally, Project Control Systems have consisted of individual and independent information processing subsystems solving specific operational problems. The individual solutions have not been necessarily compatible with each other. The systems approach suggests that every system or subsystem of project control directly affects the performance of other systems. The effective project control systems integrate the planning, scheduling, cost control, estimating, administration, status reporting, and contract effort of the project manager. The system should consist of an integrated and balanced set of methods and procedures incorporating the following elements: (1) manual and computerized systems, (2) control of forms and reports, (3) information flow, (4) records management, (5) specifications, (6) procedures, (7) standards, (8) manuals, (9) mechanization requirements, and (10) personnel organization.

The need to bring information closer to the decision maker is much more than formal information systems and using computers. It depends on vertical and horizontal communications between people in different functional groups and different levels in the organization. Traditional patterns which follow organizational lines have been deficient for making decisions in a project environment.

The final step then is the creation of new communication links, lateral relationships, between the people in the project who can carry the information to decision makers in a more timely and effective manner anywhere in the organization. Most often, management of a project takes on different forms in different organizations depending upon who the decision maker is and where the decision is made. A small project may be handled by direct contact between managers who share information for its accomplishment. A problem in the shop can be handled simply between the engineer and the foreman. From a project viewpoint, the information is at the level where the decision can be made.

When the volume of contacts between any two departments grows, it becomes more economical to set up specialized roles to handle this communication. Liaison personnel are typical examples of these specialized roles designed to facilitate communications between the departments and bypass the upward lines of communication normally involved in decision making. To illustrate this specialized role, in the steel industry when a salesperson books an order for coils, sheet, or plate steel, it is turned over to a customer service representative who maintains contact with the customer and the factory production department until final shipment is made. The customer service representative acts as the liaison between the salesperson and the factory because traditionally in steel sales there is a high volume of changes in shipment quantities, production schedules, and specifications after an order has been booked.

When projects or problems arise which involve more than several departments and their resources, the decision-making capacity of direct contacts is exceeded. Task forces are formed to handle such interdependent tasks on the horizontal basis. Task forces are made up of representatives from each of the involved departments. Some are full-time members and others are part-time members. The task force is a temporary group and exists only as long as the project may take or as the problem remains.

During the development of a computer estimating system in a large utility company, it became evident that prior to computer system design, the estimating subassembly standards required information from engineering, construction, purchasing and stores, and accounting. A task force was established to identify and categorize the labor and material for each subassembly prior to assigning account numbers, purchasing identification, and other coding needed for setting the standard. The effort took longer than originally expected, but the results were very favorable to the company. The material identification numbers were streamlined, ineffective labor practices were uncovered and corrected, surplus material was found and disposed of, and new subassemblies were designed to fill in some operating deficiencies. With completion of the project or solution of the problem, each participant returned to his or her department and normal tasks. To the extent that they are successful, task forces remove problems from higher levels of the hierarchy. They make the decisions at the lower levels in the organization. Group problem solving techniques are used as the information is available where the decisions are made.

As certain decisions consistently arise in the business organization, task forces tend to become permanent. These are labeled *standing committees* or *teams*. The group decision process becomes permanent. The task force (from the previous example) which developed the estimating subassembly standards had disbanded, but was recalled periodically to review new subassemblies which were being designed to keep up with the latest technology. They also convened to review current standards which were changing because of new material specifications or construction practices. This increase in effort resulted in establishing a standing committee to review subassemblies. The committee leader was usually the manager of the department responsible for causing the change. However, there are many organizational concerns involved with this type of team decision making, such as: (1) At what level do team members operate? (2) Who participates? (3) Who will be the leader?

Occasionally, the leadership passes from one manager to another. Consensus decisions still prevail, but occasionally when this was not possible and the protern leader could not make the decision, the information went up to the executive level for a final decision. Both consensus and executive-level decisions were costly and time consuming. Consensus decision making may be acceptable for a subassembly standards committee, however, for projects such as a million-dollar factory expansion or development of a new product line, consensus decisions are not desirable because the conditions are entirely different. These projects are usually complex efforts requiring significant contributions from different functional departments who in turn must set their own priorities and allocate their resources. Since each project has a specific objective and schedule and competes with other projects, time, resources, and productivity become critical.

Timely decision making requires full-time leadership. In most organizations, their full-time leadership is solved by creating a new integrating role called Project Coordinator, Project Engineer, Project Leader, etc. The issue with this role is to create enough power in the role to influence the decision process. Project coordinators have power because they report to the executive level even when no one reports to them. They collect information to equalize power differences with functional department heads. With preferential access to knowledge and information, the quality of joint decision is improved. Power equilization occurs only if the integrating role is staffed with someone who can exercise expert power in the form of persuasion and influence rather than exert the power of rank and authority.

As the task becomes more complex and uncertain, it becomes more difficult to exercise "expert power." The integrator must obtain more power of the formal authority type in order to be more effective in coordinating the joint decisions which had occurred at the lower levels of the organization. This becomes position power and changes the nature of the role. Labels such as Project Manager and Program Manager are found in this situation.

Unlike the integrating role, the project manager possesses formal position power, but is different from the line manager because the participants still do not report directly to him or her. The power is added by the following successive changes: the project manager has approval over budgets formed by other departments, controls the planning and budgeting process, initiates the budgeting cycle, and buys the resources from the functional groups. These steps permit the project manager to exercise considerable influence even though no one really works for her or him. The role is concerned with integration, and it exercises power through the formal power of position.

However, if this power is not sufficient to integrate the subtasks, and the creation of self-contained groups is not feasible, there is a final step. This is called the matrix organization which creates the dual authority relationship between the project manager and the functional manager. In a matrix organization, personnel assigned to the project have formal reporting relationships to the project manager. In effect, they have two bosses. They receive function direction and support from their home (functional) department, and project direction from the project manager. In theory, the project manager tells them what project work to do, and when; while the functional manager tells them how and sets the standards for technical performance. The expected result is a balance of power between the project manager and the functional line organization. The matrix covers a wide spectrum of integrating roles resulting from the wide range in the balance of power possible between project and line organizations.

Alternatives of Project Management

Project management requires a special organization, but there is no single unique project organization; rather there is a spectrum of organizational alternatives. Even the terms pure project or *matrix* do not refer to single, clearly defined organizational forms; each may have many variations. It has been proposed that organizations fit on a continuum with the functional organization and the pure project organization at the two excesses. The matrix fits in between these two extremes. However, the point is that there are not just these three alternatives but a whole spectrum of alternatives depending upon the amount of power given the so-called project manager. The continuum of matrix organizations varying from weak to strong is discussed. The balance of power tips toward the project manager in the strong matrix and toward functional management in the weak matrix.

Selecting the Right Organizational Form

How is the right organizational form of project management chosen, once the decision to implement project management has been made? The organizational form chosen must be appropriate for the company, the project or service, and its management. The type of organization needed will emerge rather clearly as answers to the following questions are obtained:

1. Is the organization ready for project management?
2. How big are the projects?
3. How complex are the projects?
4. How many projects are there?
5. What does the customer or client want?
6. What does top management want?

The answer to the question of whether the organization is ready for project management lies partly in the past history of the company or organization. Has project management been previously used in the organization, and was it successful or unsuccessful? If a previous attempt was unsuccessful, is the organization better prepared at this point in time, or will the same mistakes be made? Is the organization ready for a major reorganization? These questions concern whether management at all levels recognizes that changes are needed, and whether they are ready to accept organizational changes. It then becomes a decision as to how drastic a change will the organization tolerate without an extensive orientation program. In other words, if a rather lengthy and expensive orientation and educational program is not desired, the project organizational form should be kept as simple as possible. It might be better to start with a project coordinator or a weak matrix and wait and see how everything works out.

Does the organization have just one big project? A pure project organizational form is usually the answer for that one gigantic project, whether its an aerospace or construction project. If there are a number of rather medium-sized projects, a strong matrix is usually a better answer. Whenever there are multiple projects, a matrix should be considered, particularly if the projects are technically very complex and cross many disciplinary boundaries. A number of small projects usually suggests the use of multi project management where a single project manager has a number of small projects, none of which justify a full-time project manager. Multiproject management works best when the projects are not complex but are similar or interrelated. A multiproject manager can be very valuable in setting priorities and allocating resources.

Very complex projects, crossing many disciplinary lines, are usually best managed by a matrix organization. The advantages of the matrix are also apparent when there are a large number of projects, the principal advantage being better utilization of resources, principally people, equipment, and facilities. The type of project organization is often mandated by the client or customer, who should be accommodated if at all possible. The government and large construction companies prefer a pure project organization, particularly if it matches their own organization. They like the "mirror image" because all members of the organization know whom to contact as their equivalent in the other organization.

The most important consideration is what does top management want? After all, the boss will get her or his way, the selection of the project management organizational form should be a prerogative and responsibility of top management. In any case, since top management approval is necessary, whoever does the planning should determine what reservations and constraints top management would impose on the project organization.

The Project Manager

The selection of the right person for project manager is very important because that person constantly works with change, copes with multiple discipline groups, and deals with problems across functional lines. With conflict, the pressure of time and cost limitations, and a job that has more responsibility than authority, the project manager's success depends on personnel from different functional areas who must work as a team to accomplish the project objective.

This requires a keenly developed sense of timing, a talent to deal with human behavior in a multidisciplinary environment, and an effective leadership style.

Project managers typically employ two leadership styles in managing projects. One is characterized by going through formal organizational influence sources such as authority, reward, and punishment. The other approach focuses on the needs of team members in deriving influences for their project support.

Since project management is a function of the project, the organization, and the project manager, it should follow that these three would determine effective leadership style for managing projects — not so. The evidence shows that organizational climate is the strongest influencing factor in determining effective leadership style. What this means is that it makes little difference how complex the project, or whether the project manager reports directly to the president or another manager. If the organizational climate is good, chances are the project manager will get the job done concentrating on team member needs and support. This is slightly more than a coordinating role.

However, if the organizational climate is poor, project manager success depends on using formal authority through the hierarchical organization. In this case, the higher the position power, the more effective the results. It is important to note that extremes in organizational climate (i.e., very good or very bad) are rarely the case. Thus, the project manager normally operates in a mix, and needs to be flexible in leadership approach.

Maintaining open lines of communication and reinforcing liaison relationships between project people in the matrix and their home departments is one of the most difficult tasks for the project manager. It is incredible how much time is spent defining and discussing reporting relationships between various people assigned to a project, be it at the construction site, the home office, or between the functional departments. Who reports to whom and why? Who *should* report to whom and why? Why is somebody doing that? It is not their job! Hey, why isn't somebody doing that? It is their job! This kind of conversation is typical for an organization where there is much activity and there are many bosses flexing their hierarchical muscles. This is the type of discussion normally found in a new matrix management environment. Relationships are fluid and ambiguous; the organization appears in constant change.

In order to be effective, the pruioject manager must have a high tolerance for ambiguity and a propensity for orderliness. While the project manager needs to exercise decision-making authority, it should not be at the expense of losing matrix management flexibility or reducing the active organizational support of the functional departments. When major decisions come up, it is the project manager's primary job to determine the importance of the decision, what impact it will have on a project, who should be involved, and how much effort should be expended before the time is literally up and the decision must be made. There is much give and take in a matrix organization, with team members assuming an organizational role based on the situation as opposed to what their job description dictates. Decision-making authority in such an organizational situation gravitates to the person who has the best credentials to make the judgment. There is no single method for making this determination no strict rules or written procedures. Deciding *how* to have project decisions made rather than personally making them is the project manager's real job. This entails using a systematic approach to strengthen the decision-making process. One such method offers a series of questions which, when answered, provides the manager with insight as to whom and how many should be involved in the decision-making process.

1. Does it make a difference which course of action is adopted? How will it affect the project and impact the overall company?
2. Is there adequate information to make a proper analysis? What data is missing to put the pieces together and where can the information be obtained?
3. Who is going to be affected by the decision and is their commitment critical to its implementation?
4. If commitment is critical, will the response be in full compliance with whatever decision is made, or will there be conflict such that the decision may be L delayed, or even reversed?

The evidence indicates acceptable answers lean toward getting more information and involving more people to improve the quality of the decision. However, the project manager must weigh the involvement of people and sketchy information against time. Decisions by the project manager are necessary only when there is not enough time to get all the information required.

The project manager is the timekeeper for project decision making. When the project stakes are high, the project manager's risks are greater. Split-second timing may sound exaggerated, but since projects have specific duration and cost objectives, decisions missed are literally gone and could be very costly. The project manager is also in a good position to influence the organizational climate by personal actions. Establishing a reputation of credibility and trust through interpersonal relations will have a far-reaching effect on team motivation and morale. Single-mindedness in pursuit of project objectives, personnel planning to integrate the work flow and prevent conflict, and an honest concern for matching team member goals with project objectives will also help in establishing a more favorable organizational climate. The opportunity to perform these actions, however, rests with top management. Their support is a must for the project manager to make things happen.

Summary

Organizing for project management starts with analysis of project characteristics to determine the extent and type of organization needed for getting the job done. A variety of project management "forms," from simple liaison personnel who carry messages unobstructed across forbidden department boundaries to a pure project organization where the project manager controls her or his own "empire," are available and effective as a means for the management of projects. Also available is matrix management which refers to a continuum of organizational forms where the project personnel must relate to two bosses.

Prior to initiating the program, however, an important step is the assessment of organizational climate which is helpful in uncovering potential problems and developing the strategy for implementation. Top management involvement carries a dual responsibility: (1) commitment and visible endorsement of the program, and (2) selection of the most qualified individual for project manager. While the project manager's leadership effectiveness might be diluted by prevailing organizational climate, the "right" style can strongly influence climate and project decision making toward high team performance and successful results.

5

PROJECT MANAGER: DUTIES AND FUNCTIONS

Introduction

It is a position that can bring great rewards. But it is also a position that carries great risk because of all the unknowns that can rise up unexpectedly and bring disaster to even the best of plans. In this chapter we take a very close look at the various positions that are part of the career ladder of the project manager. We will start at the bottom of the project manager "food chain" and describe the positions that you can expect to occupy as you make your way to the top or maybe we should say as you make your way to whatever you have decided will be the top for you. This is the decision chapter for you. By the time you have completed this chapter you should have decided whether you want to be a project manager and, if so, what type of project manager you want to be. You might also be able to see beyond the position of project manager into further career progression, in either consulting or general management.

Definition of Project Manager

Simply stated, a project manager is a person who is responsible for completing a defined piece of work within an established budget, by a specific date, and with a defined set of resources (people, equipment, and facilities). Simple to say, but oh so difficult to attain. It would be simple if the work, once defined, didn't change, and if the delivery date, once set, didn't change, and if the resources, once committed, were available. But that isn't going to happen, so that is where the challenge of being a successful project manager takes its cue. We have often heard project managers say that it would be a boring job if these things didn't change, but the fact that they do change is what gets them out of bed in the morning.

Working of Project Manager

To get a good understanding of what a project manager does, we will define five types of positions on project teams. These five positions form a career path starting at the entry level and progressing to the most experienced and seasoned project management professional. Each of the five types has defined roles and responsibilities, which we will discuss in this section. We will leave for later sections the discussion of the skills needed to fulfill these roles and responsibilities.

A Team Member

For most of you, your career as a project manager will begin as a team member. At the entry level you possess some skill that is needed by the project team, and that is the reason why you have been selected as a team member. For example: You are working on a project management methodology development project, and your team is responsible for designing and developing the training curriculum that will be needed. Your job as a member of this team is to develop the slide presentation that accompanies the courses. That is all you are responsible for, and when you have finished and your work has been approved, you will have met your responsibility to the curriculum development team and will leave the project. During the times that you are actually doing work for the project, you will work under the direction of a team leader or project manager. You might be involved with the project for its entire duration, or be active only for a brief time as you deliver the work you have been asked to do.

Fundamental Understanding of Project Management

During the time you are working on the project, you might be committed full-time or for only a percentage of your time. You can also expect to be assigned to more than one project at a time. To meet your team member responsibilities, you will need a very fundamental understanding of project management only in that you have an obligation to provide periodic status information to either your team leader or to the project manager. How to do that is something you can learn on the job. There is no requirement for formal training in project management at this point. However, in anticipation of becoming a team leader someday, you should begin reading about project management at an introductory level and maybe even look into taking a three-day introductory course. If you can do that, when the time comes you will be prepared to move to team leader. Keep in mind, however, that a person moves to team leader responsibility based more on their onthe-job performance and recommendations of their team leader than on any formal training.

Team Leader

You will increase your skills through on-the-project experience and perhaps some formal training in project management at an introductory level. That will prepare you to take on limited responsibility for the work of a small team within a larger project. At the entry level you can expect team size to consist of only a few members whose expertise lies within a limited scope of work. As you learn how to direct the work of a few on a simple task, you can expect to expand to larger teams with a broader and more complex range of responsibilities.

Team leaders get good on-the-job training in project management in a somewhat protected environment. To a great extent they are insulated from the environment by the project manager. That allows them to focus on the specific activity for which they are responsible. Changes are negotiated by the project manager, and they are simply the recipient of those changes even though they may have had some role in deciding if and how to handle those changes. While you serve as team leader you can focus on learning what we call the "block and tackle" of project management. That is, you can focus on learning how to use the tools and techniques, leaving change management, politics, and communications with the stakeholders to the project manager. You will learn about project scoping, project planning (the work breakdown structure; estimating activity duration, resources, and cost; scheduling project work), reporting project progress, closing the project, and conducting a post-project audit.

Team leaders get good on-the-job training in project management given enough broadening experiences as well as formal training in project management, you will eventually reach a skill level that prepares you for an entry-level project manager position. Here you step up to a new set of challenges. Those aspects that were external to the work of the project that were the province of the project manager are now on your plate. Let's take a look at what that means.

Project Manager

To be effective your interpersonal relations, which include problem solving, decision making, and conflict resolution, are now part of your responsibility. In other words, as a team leader you could focus internally on the project, but now, as a project manager, you have to focus also on the external aspects of the project.

Team leader you could focus internally on the project: At the entry level you can expect to manage projects of limited scope and complexity and impact on the business. Such projects require a manager to have a moderate level of proficiency technical and business skills in particular in order to be successful. At the entry level you can expect to have total management responsibility for these projects. As part of your development as a project manager you will need some training. The training is not technical, however. It is more interpersonal. Course titles such as managing diversity in the workplace; how to negotiate to a win-win conclusion; managing technical people; creative problem solving; decision making; and others will be ones you should look for.

The major change that you will notice, as compared with your responsibilities as a team leader, will be the added focus external to the project. You now have direct contact with the customer, resource managers, senior management, vendors, and external contractors. Your involvement will be more managerial than technical, however. Although you may have had similar involvement as a team leader, it was probably of a limited scope and was more technical than managerial.

Senior Project Manager

At this level you are working on more complex projects that have higher visibility in the organization. Expect to leave some of your technical skills on the side, replacing them with more managerial skills. You may have done some project work as a project manager, but that will decrease as you move into the mainstream as a senior project manager. As your skill profile builds to encompass projects that are either more technical or more organizationally focused, you will take on projects of greater scope and complexity.

At the single project level you have made it once you reach senior project manager status. The organization depends on you to show leadership in the most difficult of project situations. Younger, less experienced project managers will look to you for advice and counsel. You will be mentor to many of them.

Program Manager

The distinguishing feature in this class of project manager is that program managers oversee other project managers. They will also manage the most challenging of projects in the organization. At this point in your career you have left all technical skills behind and are now a fully vested senior manager in your business unit. You are expected to contribute to the business in a proactive way within the scope of your functional responsibility. This is clearly the territory of the WOW Project.

Kinds of Projects they Manage

Type IV—Simple

Early in your career as a project manager you can expect to start with projects that are relatively straightforward, do not involve complex technologies, and have limited organizational value. For example, the installation of a server network in a field sales office, because it has been done many times over and has become rather routine, is a Type IV project. Projects such as these may seem to offer little in the way of challenge and excitement, but don't be too premature in judging them. As a beginning project manager you will have plenty of challenges and opportunities to grow and learn from such projects.

Type III—Organizationally Complex

These projects tend to use established and current technology but present a rather complex organizational environment. The complexity may arise from the fact that the project affects several business functions, is a new initiative for the enterprise, or is a combination of the two. As an example, consider the merger of two similar companies, such as two banks. The project involves establishing a standardized customer services department that will service the customers of both banks. Each bank has its own way of doing things, and it is your job to get them to agree to a single process. Sound simple? It is not. Pride of ownership and other territorial interests will have to be taken into account. As project manager you will be challenged in ways that you may never have expected.

Type II—Technically Complex

These projects are important to the enterprise but are characterized more on their technological complexity than on their organizational value. Technological complexity can arise in several ways. First, it may be a new technology or at least new to the enterprise. In any case, the enterprise does not have much experience working with it and therefore may only have a small core of professionals who understand it. The risk attendant to such projects obviously will be high. Second, the enterprise could be comfortable with the technology but not have an adequate supply of staff who understands it. A good example of this is an e-business that has companies vying to create its web site. These development efforts challenge the established processes of project management because the systems development method used on these projects is not amenable to standard project management life cycle processes. New ways of thinking about projects and development of an application that is adaptive and constantly changing are needed. These projects are clearly Type II projects.

Type I—Critical Mission

Critical mission projects tend to be on the cutting edge of technology, and a significant contributor to the business's bottom line. For both their technology and their organizational complexities, these projects demand the very best of performance from the very best project managers. As organizations struggle to redefine themselves and their businesses with new technologies driving this change every few years, they are frequently engaging in Type I projects.

What Are Your Career Choices?

Apart from being an occasional or a dedicated project manager, there are general career paths you should be familiar with. These are described below.

The Technical Track

The technical track includes such areas as construction, engineering, science, research and development, and information technology. To be a successful project manager in any of these specialty areas requires, as a minimum, an understanding of the terminology and, in most cases, a working knowledge of the field. It will not, however, generally require current practice of the technical specialty.

The area of information technology is so critical to every business activity that it deserves special mention here.

Because we all live and work in the information age, information technology and information systems are the foundation of literally every business or organizational activity in which you might be involved. That means that most projects will include an information technology component regardless of the business function or process involved. The project manager who chooses to have an information technology focus can be assured of levels of project involvement that span all four of the project types discussed earlier.

Furthermore, you are more likely to find the positions of dedicated project manager in the technical track than in the business or management tracks. This is especially true in government-related businesses and projectized organizations.

Business Track

The practice of project management is not as widespread as it is in the technical track. The occasional project manager is typically found here, while the dedicated project manager would be a rarity. The area of product development is fertile ground for project management. The need to shorten time to market is a need that can be met with good project management practices.

Management Track

Many of you are destined to rise above the rank of project manager and become a manager of project managers. This will be the case for dedicated project managers who work in projectized organizations or organizations that staff a project support office with project managers. The strong matrix structure will also have a position such as vice president of projects. All of these are opportunities for those who wish to manage project managers and have a directive responsibility for the project portfolio of the enterprise.

Demand for Project Managers

It is safe to say that the demand for project managers far exceeds the supply of qualified project managers. It is also safe to say that this situation will persist into the foreseeable future. Check out the classified ads section of any major metropolitan newspaper and it will be immediately obvious that project managers are in a seller's market. More recently, companies are posting position openings on their web sites. If you have a project manager career goal in mind and are interested in certain companies, check their web site. PMI® has a rather extensive listing of project manager position openings in a number of companies and geographic areas as well.

PMI® also publishes an annual salary survey. At the time of this writing, its most recent survey was from 1996. In that survey, the reported salary range was $50,000 to over $150,000. Obviously the range includes all levels of experience, industry, and location variables. If you are interested in more details, copies of that survey may be obtained from PMI®.

Requirement of Skills

In preparation for our discussion of the skills required to be a world class project manager, let us first look at the functions and tasks that any one of our four project manager types may be called upon to perform.

I. Planning the Project (Strategies and Tactics)

- ❐ Develops preliminary study with project team, identifying business problems, requirements, project scope, and benefits
- ❐ Identifies key project results and milestones
- ❐ Facilitates preparation of project plan and work breakdown structure
- ❐ Facilitates the estimation of time lines and project phases

II. Managing the Project

- ❐ Continually reviews project status
- ❐ Reviews work against key results criteria
- ❐ Uses systematic method for logging project status—checking against schedule
- ❐ Uses change management/request procedure

- ❒ Uses project meetings to measure progress against plan, and communicate changes and issues
- ❒ Assesses skill-needed documentation of meetings, work, conversations, and decisions
- ❒ Measures quality through testing against requirements
- ❒ Conducts project reviews and walk-through (with appropriate client involvement)

III. Leading the Project Team

- ❒ Involves team in planning
- ❒ Uses both formal and informal methods to track project status
- ❒ Recognizes individual and team accomplishments or results
- ❒ Manages performance issues in a timely manner
- ❒ Delegates tasks effectively based on understanding individual strengths and weaknesses
- ❒ Maintains open door for staff ideas and concerns

IV. Building Client Partnerships

- ❒ Involves working jointly with client in defining project goals and key results
- ❒ Works with client to assure alignment of project to overall business goals
- ❒ Listens and responds actively, and documents client needs, changes, and demands
- ❒ Implements procedures for controlling and handling change
- ❒ Develops client understanding of the system and trains in systems use
- ❒ Presents and reports periodically to client
- ❒ Establishes lines of responsibility and accountability to client

V. Targeting to the Business

- ❒ Manages in accordance with visions and values
- ❒ Links overall architecture principles
- ❒ Interfaces effectively with business systems and processes

- ❐ Plans for impacts on related systems/departments to achieve maximum efficiency
- ❐ Understands business needs, time, and cost pressures
- ❐ Keeps current with business and technology developments in competitors
- ❐ Aligns project with corporate and business priorities and direction

Competencies and Skills of the World Class Project Manager

If anyone has a foolproof method of identifying a professional who will make a competent project manager, please contact us. We can show you how to make a lot of money. In fact, it is very difficult to identify someone with the requisite competencies. There are two levels of characteristics that determine success or failure as a project manager. At the visible level are skills, whose level of mastery can be measured, and which can be acquired through training. That is the easy part. More difficult are those traits (competencies) that lie below the surface, out of visible range. We can see them in practice, but we cannot directly measure them in the sense of determining whether or not a particular person has them and, if so, to what degree. They are also the traits that are more difficult to develop through training. Some of them, in fact, may be hereditary.

According to Lyle M. Spencer and Signe M. Spencer book *Competence at Work: Models for Superior Performance*, a competency is "an underlying characteristic of an individual that is causally related to criterion-referenced effective and/or superior performance in a job or situation." In this book, five types of competency characteristics are identified. These are listed below and briefly explained.

Competency Characteristics

Motives. Those things that a person wants that will cause them to take one course of action rather than another.

Traits. Traits are characteristics that a person possesses that cause him to respond in the manner he does.

Self-Concept. Here we speak of the image that a person has of himself. Values and attitudes are a large part of a person's self-concept.

Knowledge. The awareness, data, and information that a person possesses about a specific topic or content area.

Skill. The observable and measurable performance of an individual to execute an assigned task.

Bob Wysocki 's company, Enterprise Information Insights (EII), uses an assessment tool to measure competency in eighteen different areas based on a set of observable behaviors that are related to the competencies. To establish an individual's competency level, we recommend a self-assessment be done by the individual and that several of his coworkers also provide their assessment of the individual. These coworkers might be the individual's manager, peer professionals, subordinates, and customers. Using this approach, the individual's self-assessment can be compared with their coworkers' assessments. This approach may be simplistic, but it is practical and has surfaced rather insightful conclusions regarding individual performance.

For competency assessment we define business, personal, interpersonal, and management categories. Skill assessment adds project management skills as a fifth category. Effective project managers require competencies and skills that are specific to the discipline in which the project they manage lies, and they require a set of non-discipline-specific skills that are categorized into one of the five categories described below.

Business. These competencies and skills relate to the business and business processes in general and do not involve specific business function knowledge.

Personal. Competencies and skills in this category relate to the individual. The skills do not involve another party in order to be practiced.

Interpersonal. Competencies and skills in this category relate to the individual. The skills involve at least two people, neither one of which is the manager of the other.

Management. These competencies and skills relate to all aspects of management, whether people management or work management. Also included are skills related to the performance of strategic and tactical management functions not specific to any individual.

Project Management. Project management skills span the five phases of project management: initiation, planning, organizing, controlling, and closing.

Competency Profile of the World Class Project Manager

This section discusses the competencies common to all levels of project manager. It is meant to give you a general sense of what is required to be an effective project manager and to match your current competencies against those that are required of world class project managers. What results from this examination is a gap between the competencies you have and those that you will need to add to your profile as you move through the ranks of increasing project management responsibility.

The capsule descriptions of the business, personal, interpersonal, and management competencies required to be an effective project manager. As we begin, it would be a good exercise to review this list and personally assess how your competencies measure up. The list was originally developed by the Corporate Education Center of Boston University in cooperation with several of their major corporate accounts. It has since been revised through experience with several other clients and has been adapted here with permission.

It is given here in a survey format so that you can evaluate the extent to which you practice each competency. The rating scale is 5 = Strongly Agree; 4 = Agree; 3 = Neutral; 2 = Disagree; and 1 = Strongly Disagree. Evaluate yourself on each of the competencies and follow the summary instructions given at the end.

Add the score value for each of the nineteen competency areas. The resulting scores are interpreted as follows:

Score Range	Project Manager Competency Level
4-7	Does not meet minimum competency level
8-10	Meets team leader minimum competency level
11-15	Meets project manager minimum competency level
16-18	Meets senior project manager minimum competency level
19-20	Meets program manager minimum competency level

Knowing your scores on each of the competencies will give you a rough guide as to where you should concentrate your development activities. You might want to ask your coworkers to assess your competencies and compare their responses with yours. You will discover that others do not perceive you as you perceive yourself. Their perceptions are reality regardless of how closely they agree with reality as you see it. It is a typical competency assessment report. The narrow filled rectangle is the individual's self-assessment; the filled square is the average assessment of the assessors; the unfilled rectangle is the inter-quartile range (the middle half of the data); and the end points of the solid line are the extreme observations that define the range of responses.

A Self-assessment: You have some decisions to make. And now is a good time to take stock of who you are and what you are really interested in doing. We have given you all of the data that is relevant to that decision. There are two areas of importance that we suggest you assess: your environment and you.

Your External Environment: You have to supply the realities of the environment in which you work. For example, how supportive is the organization and your manager of your development? How important is it to them? What help do they provide? To what extent are development opportunities there for you to take advantage of?

Your Internal Environment: Let's assume that you have found the environment to be supportive and conducive to your professional development. The next area of concern is you personally. How excited are you about being a project manager now that you know "the good, the bad, and the ugly" about project management? Your successful development as a project manager is totally a function of what you are willing to put into the effort. No one is going to push you. No one (except, perhaps, your mentor and a few enlightened managers) is really interested in your future. In the final analysis, it's up to you.

Your Career Path: A career path can be looked at in two ways. On the one hand it is a historical account of your professional life. On the other hand—and the one we focus on in this book—it is a look ahead at a planned course of growth and development of you as a professional. The first is a record of the past, and the second is a plan for the future.

What It Means to Have a Career Path: To have a career path simply means that you have taken a look at desirable futures and chosen the one that makes the most sense right now given where you are today. That career path will be dotted with several intermediate career goals that you will achieve along the way and culminating in a final career goal. Tomorrow you will be smarter than you are today, and those desirable futures will very likely change. The important thing is that you have defined a future and you are taking meaningful and deliberate steps toward that future.

Career Paths are Dynamic: We live and work in dynamic and changing times and we should expect our career paths to be dynamic and changing as well. Every new experience builds on its predecessor experiences and gives us new insights into the future. Opportunities arise and cause career interests to change (either temporarily or permanently), and hence career paths to change.

Conclusion

You now have a complete picture of the project manager. You know what is done in each type of project manager role. You know what kinds of projects are managed as a project manager grows professionally. You know what competencies and skills they must possess to be successful at each stage of their professional development, and you have evaluated yourself against those standards. You have also taken a first look at what it means to have a career path.

6

PROJECT MANAGER: ROLE AND FUNCTIONS

Introduction

The type of project you want to manage will require a set of skills particular to that type of project. The good news is that these skills can be acquired with patience and initiative on your part. We'll describe exactly what those skills are, give you a tool to measure where you stand with respect to those skills, and then in later chapters help you develop a plan to acquire them.

Project management is the "in" thing at the present time. More and more people are becoming project managers. Certificates and degree programs are being offered by colleges and universities throughout the country. Conferences are cropping up at an unprecedented rate. You would think we had discovered the holy grail of management.

Yet people have been managing projects for thousands of years. The first project managers built the Pyramids; Stonehenge; the Maya, Aztec, and Inca temples; the Roman roads; the Great Wall of China; and many other marvels.

So the discipline is very old. Why all the fuss, then? Perhaps because we have finally realized how useful the skills of project management can be. Perhaps it is because organizations are trying to run "lean and mean," by downsizing, right-sizing, or whatever. Perhaps it is because our world is so turbulent today, and we are trying to bring order out of chaos. No doubt all of these are factors.

In any case, one indicator of the growth in project management is the growth of the professional association the Project Management Institute (PMI). In 1970 they had approximately 5,000 members, after twenty years of existence. In April 2000, the figure had reached 57,000, and approximately 1,300 new members are being added every month. Likewise, professional associations are being formed in Russia, Europe, Australia, and elsewhere.

Another indicator is the growing number of master's degree in project management programs and the large enrollments that they are experiencing. George Washington University started a program in September 1996, and by the following September their enrollment had already reached 150. As of January 2000 *Peterson's Annual Guide* listed over twenty institutions offering advanced degrees in project management.

Finally, a significant indicator of how important project management is may be given by the number of project scheduling software programs (of which there are more than one hundred PC products alone) that have been sold. Microsoft, with over 80 percent market share, has sold over 1 million copies of Microsoft Project. This means that at least a million individuals have felt a need to try to schedule projects. No doubt there are many more who manage projects without benefit of any scheduling software. In seminars taught by Jim Lewis, only about one-third of participants are using software regularly. If this ratio holds true nationwide, then perhaps 3 million people are actually managing projects without using scheduling software. Of course, this is totally speculative. All we can say is that there is definitely a lot of interest in the profession.

Is It All Just a Passing Fad?

For the United States, it is reasonable to ask if this interest in project management is just a passing fad. After all, we have tried all kinds of "quick fixes" since 1980, when quality circles became all the rage. You would be hard-pressed to find many quality circles in the United States today. Will project managers also become extinct when the candy coating wears off the pill? If so, should you invest in a career that might not take you anywhere?

We have talked with a number of experts in the field, and most of them believe that it is not just a fad. The reason is that project management is a specialized discipline, providing skills needed to manage a project successfully. Since it is hard to imagine a world without projects, it seems likely that the profession will endure.

A better question might be, then, "Do I want to be a dedicated, fulltime project manager or an occasional project manager?" We will define the occasional and the dedicated project manager in this chapter and help you answer this question. For now, we will discuss what project management is all about for the occasional and for the full-time, dedicated project manager.

What Is a Project?

Before you know if you are a project manager, you need to understand the difference between projects and non projects. Projects come in all shapes and sizes. There are two definitions that capture the essence of all projects. One is that a project is a job consisting of multiple tasks that is done one time. It should have well-defined starting and ending times, a defined scope of work, and a budget of some kind.

Another definition, by Dr. J. M. Juran, is that a project is a problem scheduled for solution. This definition supports the previous one, and makes us realize that when we do a project, we are solving a problem for the organization. However, we don't necessarily mean "problem" in a negative sense. Developing a new product is a positive kind of problem. So is moving to a new facility.

If you have any experience managing projects, you no doubt recognize that a lot of so-called projects do not conform to the first definition. Rather than having well-defined starting and ending points, they seem to evolve from some vague idea to full-blown project status, and like the Energizer Bunny, they also keep on going and going and going.

The problem caused by a project evolving from a vague idea into a full-blown effort is that proper planning is usually not done. And, if no proper plan is made, then management of the project is likely to suffer.

What Is Project Management?

Project management is really not much more than organized common sense. To be more specific, project management is facilitation of the planning, scheduling, and controlling of activities needed to accomplish objectives. These objectives include cost, performance, time, and scope. The relationship among them is given by this equation

$C = f(P, T, S)$

The equation means, "Cost is a function of Performance, Time, and Scope."

Project managers are always making trade-offs between these four objectives. It is very common that senior managers try to assign values to all four of them, yet we know that in an equation with four variables, only three can have values assigned. The fourth will be whatever the equation says it will be. This means that project managers will often have to negotiate with others to establish a balanced cost equation. In many cases earlier commitments of all four objectives will have been made, and unfortunately that negotiation will not happen. The project manager is now placed in a very difficult position. If she says no, she might be accused by senior management of not being a team player. If she says yes, she might set herself up for an eventual failure.

The answer lies in formally proposing and prioritizing feasible alternatives from which senior management must pick one. In other words, to simply say yes to an impossible situation is not acceptable. Just make sure it really is an impossible situation and that no amount of creativity will resolve it before you push back to senior management. You are creating a potentially embarrassing position, and you might be the one who is embarrassed.

Types of Project Manager Roles

There are two types of project managers we will consider in this book. They are the occasional project manager and the dedicated or fulltime project manager.

The Occasional Project Manager

Most of you will practice project management in this setting. For some of you it will have been a conscious choice to do so, and for others a condition of employment. In either case your primary responsibility will be to a business function or process, and you will use project management as one of many tools to meet your responsibilities. Even though project management is not your principal avocation, it is an important part of what you do. Remember, Tom Peters believes that we will all become project managers of one type or another, and that project management may only be a small part of what we do but it might also be a major part of what we do. In any case, you will want to develop some level of proficiency, so this book will be important to your professional development whatever that level of proficiency might be.

Tools of Project Management

There are no doubt more part-time project managers than there are full-time managers. If you run projects occasionally, the natural question to ask is, "Just how much time should I invest in learning the tools of project management?" Certainly you wouldn't likely want to get a master's degree in project management if you only manage projects occasionally. You might not even want a noncredit certificate. But you should definitely know the essential tools of project management. These include tools for planning, scheduling, and controlling projects. The basic tools that anyone managing projects should be familiar with. Whether you use them regularly is not too important. You can always choose not to use tools that you know, but you can't use tools that you don't know about.

These tools can be learned in a three-day seminar on project management. If you have not had such a course, you should study prospective course outlines to see that they cover these topics. Further, you should be wary of one- and two-day programs that promise to make you a professional project manager. It takes at least three days to cover these methods in detail, since you need practice in applying them. A well-designed program will involve some skill-building exercises that have you apply the tools as you learn them.

You might also want to learn these tools by reading and actively using a good practice-oriented book on project management. For example, you might adopt Bob Wysocki *Effective Project Management*, or Jim Lewis book *Project Planning, Scheduling and Control*. Both present project management with an applications and "how-to" approach.

One trap that occasional project managers often confront is that they are expected to be working project managers. This means they are expected to perform some of the work that their team members also do. This can be okay on very small projects, but at some point the work will take priority over managing the job, and managing will suffer. When this happens, you need to ask that you be relieved of the work responsibility so that you can concentrate on your managing responsibilities. This does not mean that you will be a full-time project manager forever, but for the duration of this project, it may be necessary. Otherwise, at review time, you will be evaluated on managing, and your supervisor may tell you that your managing leaves something to be desired.

One obvious advantage to being an occasional project manager is that you have a chance to see if you want to be a full-time project manager. As is true of any profession, there are pros and cons about project management. Project management does have high visibility in a lot of companies, and offers a bridge between lower level positions and consulting or executive level jobs. In fact, there is some reason to believe that project management may become the route to the top in the future. We discuss a career model that shows how project managers are positioned in a comprehensive career ladder. That model demonstrates how project management can be a goal in and of itself as well as an intermediate stop on the way to either consulting or senior management positions.

However, project managers often suffer a great deal of stress, so "If you can't stand the heat, get out of the kitchen," as the old saying goes. We have found a lot of people who *want to be managers* but don't really *want to manage*. There is a big difference. If you are an occasional project manager and are trying to make up your mind whether to go for a full-time position, this book should be especially useful.

Dedicated or Fulltime Project Manager

There is a philosophy followed in some organizations that says if you can manage one project, you can manage any project. You might work for this type of organization and find it to be as much, if not more of a challenge than working as an occasional project manager.

Your organization may be structured along the lines of a projectized organization, in which case project managers are dedicated project managers. Organizationally they may be attached to a project office or report to a vice president of projects. They move from project to project. When one project is finished, they are reassigned to another project. Although these projects might be in the same discipline, that is not always the case. That is the job of the dedicated project manager. The dedicated project manager will most often be found in a projectized organization.

If you already are a full-time project manager, or aspire to be one, the question would be whether you want to continue in project management for the foreseeable future. If you do, should you get an advanced degree, a certificate, or just continue as you are? This book is designed to help you make these decisions. There are a lot of organizations looking for professional project managers. Some are even insisting that you have Project Management Institute (PMI) certification (not to be confused with a certificate in project management). We will discuss PMI™ certification later in this chapter. A project manager told Jim Lewis recently that he tried to get a job that paid $100,000 a year, but was turned down because he did not have his PMI™ certification. So professional project managers have a bright future at the moment, and this should not change unless there becomes a glut in the market.

Project Manager Food Chain

Whether you are an occasional or dedicated project manager, there is another way to slice the project manager pie. There are several stages of professional growth for the project manager. It starts out when you first realized that you wanted to be a project manager. We call these the "wanna-bes" and start them at the entry-level position that we call team member. The specific entry-level skill profile that you will need in order to be a team member. As you might guess, this will be a minimal set of project management skills and will encompass mainly personal and interpersonal skills as well as business and general management skills. Team members are generally chosen based on their technical skills rather than on any project management skills they might have. As you continue your participation as a team member you will eventually acquire a basic set of project management skills either through on-the-job experience or formal training. This will prepare you to move to the next level, which we call a team leader. This is a fancy name for an individual who manages a piece of work within the project. As team leader you will often have one or two subject matter specialists working with you on an activity within the project. We define the specific entry-level skills that you will need in order to be a team leader. You will have additional assignments as team leader that will move you from simple to more complex types of assignments. Along the way your team size may increase and give you more experience working with larger groups of people on more complex activities. This process repeats itself with additional project management skills acquisition on your part as you move along a defined path from team leader to project manager to senior project manager to program manager. Did you ever expect the career path of the project manager to be this extensive? As you will see, it provides a clearly defined path that will give you a foundation on which to build a sound professional development plan. Depending on your interest in retaining your focus as a technical expert, you may trade off with your project manager aspirations. For example, if you want to be an internal consultant, recognized for your specialization, you might aspire to be a team leader. Your contribution to a project will be to lead a team of others in your area of specialization.

This can be a very challenging and rewarding experience for those who want to be a specialist and yet have some involvement with project management.

PMI™ Certification

PMI™ is the major professional association of project managers in the United States. Its membership reached 54,000 in January 2000 and continues to increase at a rate of about 25 percent per year. There is every reason to believe that that growth rate will continue into the foreseeable future. Of those 54,000 members, over 15,000 had achieved certification as a Project Management Professional (PMP™). To achieve this professional certification, an individual has to pass a written exam and demonstrate practice of the profession for a period of two years. The exam tests your knowledge in nine areas, called the Project Management Body of Knowledge (P M B O K ™).

There is also an annual continuing education requirement needed to maintain certification. That can be met by attending conferences or participating in additional seminars and workshops. Many companies are now requiring PMI™ certification as a condition of moving along their project manager career path. You should find out how your company views such certification and what they are willing to do to support employees who are interested in seeking it.

As was stated previously, the PMI™ is the professional association for project managers. They have a program to certify project managers as professionals. The designation that follows your name is PMP™, which means Project Management Professional.

As was mentioned, some companies are requiring that their project managers become certified. Others are insisting that consulting firms must employ PMP^tm^s if they are going to do contracting or consulting for them. For more information on PMP^tm^ certification, contact the PMI^tm^. Many of the university certificate programs are designed to help people prepare for the PMP^tm^ certification exam. If you intend to become certified, this would be an important consideration in selecting a certificate program to attend. PMI^tm^ has chapters throughout the United States that offer certification study groups as well, so you can obtain study materials from PMI^tm^ and then attend a study group to prepare for the exam.

Career Progression Model

To further put the project manager career paths into perspective, we have constructed a model that illustrates the options open to you. The first thing to note about this model is that project management positions are the staging point for either of two career paths. One is a consultant track that allows you to continue working as an individual contributor or team leader but with increasing responsibilities having enterprise-wide scope. The other is a management track that allows you to move farther up in the organization by changing your job focus from the management of work (project manager) to the management of people (general manager). In both cases, however, you should expect to pass through a stage where you have some level of project management responsibility. That responsibility can range anywhere from team leader through program manager. Note also that project management positions are excellent preparation for either of the three further career paths. During your tenure as a project manager you will discover whether your professional goals lie within project management or whether you aspire to positions as an individual contributor (consultant track) or to positions in people management (management track).

Good, the Bad, and the Ugly

We feel compelled at this early stage to tell you that being a project manager is easy, but being a successful project manager is very difficult. It isn't because you are not appropriately skilled for the job but rather because you face a very difficult, ever-changing, and usually hostile environment. This topic is so important that we have devoted an entire chapter to it. We were fortunate to recruit Doug DeCarlo, who at the time was a senior consultant for the ICS Group in Norwalk, Connecticut, to share his expertise on this hostile environment and write for us. For now it is sufficient to briefly mention that there are at least three causes for this hostile environment as discussed below.

Unrealistic Targets

Being competitive in today's fast-paced business world means getting there first, with the best and at the best price. Today's businesses are forced, by nature, to be aggressive, and that aggressiveness translates into project requirements and schedules that are often unrealistic. Someone once said: "If you can't meet the customer's requirements, they will find someone who will." If you expect to succeed as a project manager, you must understand the situation you are placed in and deal with it in the best way possible.

Lack of Resources

One of the realities of downsizing is that many of the people are gone, but somehow their work didn't go away. That means that the survivors are overburdened with work, and this translates into problems for the project manager. As project manager you do not have line authority over your team members. You simply manage their work, and this will require sound leadership skills from you. You are in a position of having to influence without authority. Your team members are organizationally accountable to their line manager, who has to deal with several competing and often conflicting requests for their time.

Here the project manager must function as negotiator, and that situation creates uncertainty for them. They never really know when they can count on a resource to be available on the agreed scheduled date and for the agreed level of effort over an agreed length of time. Again, if you expect to succeed as a project manager, you must understand the resource contention problem that you are placed in and deal with it in the best way possible. That will draw upon your skills as a creative problem solver and negotiator.

Is This a Losing Situation?

To be frank, it often is. You may find that discouraging, but that's reality. You will need a firm resolve to be a project manager, and that means you will need to be well-prepared for the battle ahead. We have put into the pages of this book all of the wisdom and experience we have gathered over the thirty-five years that each of us has been involved in project management. That is the best we can do for you. The rest will be up to you.

Types of Projects

We look deeper into the types of projects you will encounter you will realize that they offer you a rich source of development opportunities. There is a natural progression of projects in terms of technical and organizational complexity, and that progression fits neatly into our career progression model for project managers. Make no mistake, there are a number of possibilities for you to tap into as you look for on-the-project training and development opportunities.

The project classification model we use in this book was originally developed by the Center for Project Management (CPM), a California project management consulting and training company. It is a robust model that defines four types of projects based on an assessment of the projects' organizational and technical complexity. We present a mapping of these project types to project manager skill profiles. You will be able to evaluate yourself against these profiles. This establishes the baseline from which we will show you how to plan your own professional development program.

Technically Complex Projects

Technical complexity refers to the technology that will be used in the project. Think of technology in the broadest sense of the term. In other words, engineering, research and development, science, construction, medicine, the biological sciences, and others are included. If the technology is well established or otherwise in common use in the organization, the project will be classified as simple from a technical standpoint. That means that few problems, if any, will be expected. The project will not be at risk for any technical reasons.

If it is a new technology or is otherwise unfamiliar to the organization, the project will be classified as complex from a technical standpoint. Technical complexity can also arise when a known technology is being applied in a new or unique way. If the staff needed to use the technology are scarce or not fully qualified, that may contribute to the technical complexity. Obviously such projects will be at risk and have a high probability of failure.

Organizationally Complex Projects

Organizational complexity refers to the environment in which the project will be undertaken. If the project involves only one function or unit within the organization, affects only a few processes or procedures, and does not require considerable cultural adjustment or change, it will be classified as organizationally simple. On the other hand, if it represents considerable change, is highly controversial, or affects several processes or procedures, it will be classified as organizationally complex. The stability of the organization will also contribute to organizational complexity.

Conclusion

At this point we have given you a high level look at projects, project management, and the project manager. You understand that there are two types of project manager, occasional or dedicated, and that each has a very different role in the organization. You also understand that there is a career ladder that progresses to project management and beyond into either consulting or people management. You might choose to have project management as a career goal or use it as a staging area for more professional growth.

7

Profiles of Project Managers

Introduction

Project managers can be found everywhere. As pointed out earlier, some were placed in the position, while others chose it voluntarily. Whichever the case, there are a number of situations we would like to bring to your attention as you contemplate possible futures.

Profiles of Project Managers

Just what kind of person makes a good project manager? Is there a way to tell beforehand if you have what it takes, or do you have to spend time finding out the hard way?

We have been asked many times what characteristics we believe are most important for a project manager to have, and have never hesitated to say, "Good people skills." The reason is very simple: Project managers often have considerable responsibility, yet seldom have any authority over the people on their project teams. This means that the only way they will get anything done is through the exercise of influence, persuasion, negotiation, and maybe a little begging at times. So interpersonal skills are at the top of our list.

We have also asked participants in our seminars to list the qualities they want to see in a project manager, and the following table shows what they consistently say.

Attributes of Project Managers

Good listener	Mutual ownership
Supportive	Buffer to rest of organization
Organized	Visible leadership
Clears roadblocks	Technical knowledge
Mutual respect	Fair
Team builder	Flexible
Knows own limitations	Open-minded
Sense of humor	Delegates
Gives feedback	Honest and trustworthy
Good decision maker	Understanding
Follows up	Challenges team to do well
Shares experience	Knows strengths and weaknesses of team members

Notice the small number of items in the list that have to do with the technical and administrative aspects of project management. These are not top priorities for people. Rather, what is important to them is what we would call the *character* of the manager. She is trustworthy, shows mutual respect for co-workers, is a good listener, and so on. Without these qualities, people are not eager to follow your lead, and a project manager must be a leader of the team.

HBDI and Project Managers

Elsewhere we have discussed the Herrmann Brain Dominance Instrument (HBDI), which measures thinking preferences. We wondered what kind of profile would be typical for project managers, so we asked the Herrmann International people to pull the profiles of all the project managers they had in their database. They had 1,250 profiles of people who reported being project coordinators (the official title used by Herrmann International to classify this occupation). The overall average profile for the group was almost perfectly square.

What does that tell us? It says that the kind of people who become project managers come in all shapes and sizes (profile-wise). Some are conceptual thinkers. Some love doing detail work. Some are analytical, and some are more interpersonal. There is no dominant profile that says "this person will be an ideal project manager."

In fact, you can see that thinking in all four quadrants is necessary in managing a project. When you are developing project strategy, you need conceptual thinking (yellow, or the D-Quadrant). When you start developing an implementation plan, you need green, or B-Quadrant thinking. During execution you have to deal with lots of people issues, which requires red, or C-Quadrant thinking. And when problems exist, you may need a good shot of analytical thinking (blue, or the B-Quadrant).

Ned Herrmann suggested that good chief executive officers could benefit by having square profiles, because this would make them better able to translate between the quadrants. This is important, since they have to deal with people in all four quadrants.

We believe the same can be said for project managers. You have to deal with people whose thinking preferences fall in all four quadrants, so it would be nice to have a balanced profile yourself.

Most of us aren't that lucky. So we have to cover those quadrants where we have low preferences by making sure someone on our team does the thinking required—or else we have to force ourselves to do the required thinking, even though it is not our strong preference. Remember—we all have a whole brain, we just prefer to exercise certain modes of thinking more than others. It's not that we can't do it; it's just that we don't prefer some modes.

Interviews with Project Managers

To help you get a better picture of what it means to be a project manager, we have interviewed five project managers from different walks of life. The summaries of those interviews are given below.

A Manager of Project Managers

In preparing this book, we interviewed a number of managers of project managers and asked them this question: "What do you consider important characteristics of a good project manager?" The responses we received are as follows.

George Hollins is director of design and construction services at the University of Iowa, in Iowa City. George did not hesitate to respond.

"People skills! We give our biggest and most important projects to the project managers who can deal best with people. We sometimes think that a person who is a really good architect will be a good project manager, but it isn't necessarily true."

He said they actually had to take one fellow out of the project management job and put him back into a technical job because he had a way of irritating people with whom he dealt. And that included not only members of the project team, but customers as well. "He just didn't know how to get along with people," said Hollins.

George himself first earned a degree in civil engineering, then went on to get a degree in business administration. He considers project management to be a key to the success of the projects they manage, which are to build classroom buildings for the university. He has invested heavily in training his staff in those principles. He plans to get his PMP™ in the near future.

Long-time Project Manager

Bob Dudley managed projects in paper mills for nearly thirty years before he retired recently. He was also an operations manager for about six years, so he has seen "both sides of the fence." Bob earned a degree from the University of Florida in construction, but scheduling by using the critical path method was fairly new at the time, so he had to learn much of it later on the job. Before he retired, he passed his PMPtm certification, because he views project management as his profession. He now consults on and teaches project management.

Bob says, "You have to look at a project as an integrated whole. Many project managers are either estimators or schedulers, and they forget the big picture." He added, "Communication skills are of utmost importance. Some of the project managers I have known can't write a coherent sentence."

"People skills are numbers one and two," he said. "You can't get the cooperation of superintendents, mechanics, and other people affected by the project without them. You also need a field presence. You need to know what you're talking about. You can't b.s. them. And you can't run a project from an office. You have to get into the field."

He went on to tell about a project manager who was having trouble getting people to come to meetings to sign drawing changes. He started taking a box of doughnuts and a big pot of coffee to the superintendent's office for the Tuesday morning meeting. People started coming in.

As Bob said, it might seem trivial, but the project manager did something that showed a willingness to give them something in return for their help, and they responded by giving that help.

An Engineering Project Manager

Harold Arnison has a BS in industrial technology and has worked as an electrical engineer for eighteen years, doing product development. Those products are medical electronics, which require FDA approval and so must be of the highest caliber.

The company he works for was recently acquired by General Electric, one of the few companies that has a dual career ladder. Before the acquisition, however, Harold earned his master's in project management from Kellogg Graduate School, because he was intrigued by the discipline and wanted to improve his skills. He is now an adviser of project managers. He plans to get his PMP™ certification soon.

"The ability to work with people of all personalities is a key competency," Harold said. "We have to work with very diverse groups. We have people with medical degrees, technical degrees, and no degrees at all, and we must be able to work smoothly with them."

He went on to say that a project manager must have a structured approach to his or her work. They must be able to develop a good plan, yet remain flexible so that they can "roll with inevitable changes" that affect every project. "They have to be able to develop a schedule for unscheduled events," he added, and he emphasized that "these are far easier to deal with if you have a plan in the first place."

He said, "Everything we do is under project management control. However, we don't use money as a metric as much as we should, but we are going that way." He was referring to earned value tracking.

His advice to wanna-be project managers: "Realize that you must leave your technical skills alone. Don't take on a significant part of design work. If you do, you fall into the managing-versus-doing trap, and the managing always suffers."

An Example from India

A few years ago, Jim Lewis was in India teaching project management, and a participant told him this story. It seems that a large road construction project was having serious problems. Working conditions were bad, the food the workers were fed was substandard, and living conditions at the site were abominable. (The workers lived in tents at the construction site, as it was in a remote location.) The result was that morale was low, motivation was nonexistent, and work was going at a snail's pace.

The project manager and his assistants stayed at a nice hotel in a town some distance from the site, and commuted back and forth. This added to the low morale of workers. Fortunately, the project manager figured out what was wrong and took steps to correct the problem. He moved to the site, together with his assistants. Living conditions for the workers quickly improved. The food improved. And with it came an improvement in worker morale, motivation, and performance.

A Young Female Project Manager

Carol asked not to be identified, but gave us permission to include her comments as follows. She is twenty-five years old, an engineer, and is managing a project in which her team is in the Northeast, whereas she is located in the Southeast. In managing this high-tech project, she had two strikes against her. First, the team is at a remote location. Second, because of her age and gender, they saw her as an interference, or perhaps even worse, as a threat. In any case, things did not go well at the beginning.

Carol explained that she simply visited the team monthly to let them know that she was not there to interfere with their work, or to direct them in how to do it, but to be a resource for them. If there was anything they needed, she would do her best to get it for them.

After several months of approaching them in this way, they began to accept her, and in the end they fully accepted her role as the project manager. Had she not won them over by adopting the helper or facilitator role, she may never have been successful in managing the project.

This example again illustrates the need for dealing with the human side of the equation. Her expertise as an engineer counted for very little. It let them know that she at least could understand their work, but that was all. Furthermore, her role as project manager was initially rejected, and her attempt to plan, schedule, and control the project never would have worked if she hadn't gained their acceptance of her. What is significant is that Carol actually exercised the attributes of a leader to win over the members of this team.

"They Don't Know How to Manage Projects"

We interviewed Julian Stubbs, CEO of the Dowell// Stubbs advertising agency, located in Stockholm, about project management in an ad agency. "I'm having a terrible time finding project managers," Julian said. "I can find plenty of individuals who have good technical skills. They can do artwork, write copy, and manage accounts, but they don't know how to manage projects."

We asked him what he considers to be vital skills for project managers in an ad agency. His reply was immediate: "To be able to manage chaos, to respond to quick turnaround requests, to meet deadlines, and to smooth ruffled feathers." He went on: "Egos in advertising and marketing people can be pretty high, and they don't always take kindly to being 'managed' in the first place. If you don't deal with them with kid gloves, you will never get the job done."

Julian went on to say that they don't do highly structured scheduling, using PERT/CPM techniques, but every project is deadline driven, and because of the creative nature of the work, it is always tempting for people to say that it is hard to meet deadlines, but it is mandatory, and creativity can't be sacrificed in the process. The pressure can be enormous, and only a person who can deal with that pressure will be successful in such an environment.

Interview Questions

Following are some of the kinds of questions that are asked of project manager candidates. You should find these helpful in thinking about your own qualifications. They will also help you prepare for an upcoming interview.

- ❐ What does project management mean to you?
- ❐ What was a valuable lesson you learned from a project, and how did you (or will you) apply it to future projects?
- ❐ What do you do to handle conflicts within a project team?
- ❐ Tell us about one success and one failure you've had on projects.
- ❐ Why do you feel you're qualified for this position?
- ❐ How would you handle a project that's off track or stalled?
- ❐ What characteristics do you bring to this position?
- ❐ How do you deal with a non-team player or difficult team member?
- ❐ If priorities change, what do you do?
- ❐ How do you see yourself in the role of project manager?

- What do you do when there is a conflict about the P, C, T, S targets?
- How would you handle misinformation from team members?
- Describe what a successful project is.
- Suppose there is a change in expectations of a key stakeholder to your project. What would you do?
- What do you do when you feel that senior management is setting unobtainable project goals?
- In a project in which team efforts seem to be heading in the wrong direction, what actions would you take to correct the situation?

Conclusion

The message must be clear by now: Technical skills are less important than the ability to deal effectively with people, regardless of the field you are in. That doesn't mean that you can manage projects that you know nothing about. Remember, you can't b.s. field people—or engineers or scientists, or programmers. However, you need not be a technical expert; nor can you be on a multidisciplinary project. You must be able to communicate, negotiate, lead, influence, manage conflict, and deal with politics. You have to understand people. And you need to care about them. If you don't care about people, they will sense it, and will not readily go the extra mile for you.

8

Duties and Job of the Project Manager

Introduction

The job has aspects and problems which go beyond those of the usual line or functional manager. The major difference between line and project management can be found in the project manager's necessary preoccupation with the integration of her or his project. However, a review of the literature provides remarkably little useful information indicating exactly how this important process of systems integration is conducted. This chapter will investigate the integration process and indicate to prospective project managers how they can initiate the process.

Tasks and Duties

It is a management axiom that the overall job of every manager is to create within the organization an environment which will facilitate the accomplishment of its objectives. Certainly the job of the project manager fits this role very well. In addition, every manager is responsible for the generally accepted managerial functions of planning, organizing, staffing, directing, and controlling. Since every manager has these functions, how does the job of the project manager differ from that of the line or discipline manager?

The project management concept is based on vesting in a single individual the sole authority for the planning, resource allocation, direction and control for the accomplishment of a single, time-, and budget-limited enterprise. But this statement does not indicate any major difference between the job of the project manager and the line or discipline manager.

Problem Area

The project manager has one particular problem which is intensified in comparison with the similar problem of the line or discipline manager. Any complex project must be subdivided into tasks that are capable of accomplishment. The result is a multitude of separate tasks. These tasks are then performed by specialized functional- or discipline-oriented organizations as appropriate. The resulting complex matrix organization gives the project manager many more organizational and project interfaces to manage. Archibald indicates that "the basic concept of interface management is that the project manager plans and controls (manages) the points of interaction between various elements of the project, the product, and the organizations involved."

These interfaces are a problem for the project manager, since whatever obstacles are encountered are usually the result of two organizational units going in different directions. An old management cliché says that all the really difficult problems occur at organizational interfaces. The problem is complicated by the fact that the organizational units are usually not under direct management, and some of the important interfaces may be outside of the company or enterprise.

Interface Management

Interface management consists of identifying, documenting, scheduling, communicating, and monitoring interfaces related to both the product and the project. Interfaces are of many kinds. Archibald divides them into two types product and project, and then further divides them into subgroups, of which management interfaces are a major division. The problem of the overall project/functional interface is thoroughly discussed by Cleland and King who point out the complementary nature of the project and the functional or discipline-oriented organizations. "They are inseparable and one cannot survive without the other."

Project management, however, is more than just this management interface, it involves three types of interfaces which the project manager must continually monitor for potential problems: (1) personal interfaces, (2) organizational interfaces, and (3) system interfaces.

Personal Interfaces

These are the "people" interfaces within the organization which are working to carry out the project. Whenever two people are working on the same project we have a potential for personal problems and even conflict. If the people are both within the same line or discipline organization, the project manager has limited authority, but can demand that the line supervision resolve the personal problem or conflict. If the people are not in the same line or discipline organization, the project manager enters into the role of a mediator, with the ultimate alternative of insisting that line management resolve the problem or remove one or both of the individuals from the project team. Personal interface problems become even more troublesome and difficult to solve when they involve two or more managers.

Organizational Interfaces

Organizational interfaces are the most troublesome since they involve not only people, but also varied organizational goals and conflicting managerial styles and aspirations. Each organizational unit has its own objectives, its own disciplines or specialties, and its own functions. As a result of these differences in organizational units, each has its own jargon, often difficult for other groups to understand or appreciate. It is thus apparent that misunderstanding and conflict can easily occur at the interfaces. These interfaces are more than purely management interfaces since much day-to-day contact is at the working level. Purely management interfaces exist when important management decisions, approvals, or other actions will affect the project. Organizational interfaces also involve units outside the immediate company or project organizations such as the customer, subcontractors, or other contractors on the same or related systems.

System Interfaces

System interfaces are the product, hardware, facility, construction, or other types of nonpeople interfaces inherent in the system being developed or constructed by the project. These will be interfaces between the various subsystems in the project. The problem is intensified because the various subsystems will usually be developed by different organizational units. As pointed out by Archibald, these system interfaces can be actual physical interfaces existing between interconnecting parts of the system, or performance interfaces existing between various subsystems or components of the system. System interfaces may actually be schedule milestones involving the transmission of information developed in one task to another task by a specific time, or the completion of a subsystem on schedule.

The project manager's problem is that of interface management. What is done to solve this problem can be described by the more general term -*systems integration.*

The Integration Process

Systems integration is related to what Koontz and O'Donnell call "the essense of management-coordination, or the purpose of management is the achievement of harmony of individual effort toward the accomplishment of group goals." However, doesn't every manager have this function? Yes, but the project manager has to be preoccupied with it. The project manager's major responsibility is for assuring that a particular system or activity is assembled so that all of the components, parts, subsystems, and organizational units fit together as a functioning, integrated whole according to plan. Carrying out this responsibility comprises the function of systems integration. Integration is an action that is important to the success of any project whether hardware is involved or not. Any project involving many people, many organizational units, and many subsystems must be carefully and thoroughly integrated if the system is going to fit together as projected.

The management function of integration was identified and described by Lawrence and Lorsch. They pointed out that with the rapid advances in technology and the increased complexity of systems to be managed, there is an increased need both for greater specialization (differentiation) and for tighter coordination (integration). An effective manager has a need for both; however, since these two needs are essentially antagonistic, one can usually be achieved only at the expense of the other.

It has been suggested that the ideal high-performance manager falls on the arrow midway between differentiation and integration, and probably is typical of high-performance top management. It is also true that line or discipline management usually falls closer to the differentiation arrow, and that the project manager falls closer to the integration arrow. This model illustrates the need for the project manager as integrator.

The role of the project manager in the matrix organization has been analyzed by Galbraith, Lawrence and Lorsch, Lorsch and Morse and Davis and Lawrence. They point out that the horizontal communication in a matrix organization requires an open, problem-solving climate. However, as pointed out by Galbraith, when the subtasks in an organization are greatly differentiated, a matrix structure may be required to achieve integration. The integrator coordinates the decision processes across the interfaces of differentiation. The project manager as the integrator is necessary to make the matrix organization work. Problem solving and decision making are critical to the integration process since most project problems occur at subsystem or organizational interfaces. The project manager is the only person in the key position to solve such interface problems. The project manager provides "(1) a single point of integrative responsibility, and (2) integrative planning and control." The project manager is faced with three general types of problems and the subsequent necessity for decision making:

1. Administrative problems usually involving the removal of road blocks or the setting of priorities. A major effort is usually necessary to resolve organizational conflicts involving people, resources, or facilities.
2. Technical problems which necessitate making key decisions, deciding on scope changes, and making key tradeoffs among cost, schedule, or performance. Decisions are necessary to select between technical alternatives which impact project performance.
3. Customer or client problems which involve interpretation of and conformance to specifications and regulatory agency documents.

It is just the first step for the project manager to recognize that his or her primary job is that of integrator. It is then important that the project manager has a good idea as to how to accomplish the total process of integration. What exactly should be done to assure that the process of integration takes place?

Critical Actions of Integration

The integration process is difficult to separate from general good management practice. However, the integration process consists of a number of critical actions which the project manager must initiate and continually monitor. In most cases the project manager is the single point of integrative responsibility, and is the only person who can initiate these actions. Among the most important of these actions are:

1. Plan for integration.
2. Develop integrated work-breakdown structure, schedule, and budget.
3. Continually review and update project plan.

4. Assure project control and adherence to project plan.
5. Assure design for an integrated system.
6. Resolve conflict situations.
7. Remove roadblocks.
8. Set priorities.
9. Make administrative and technical decisions across interfaces.
10. Solve customer or client problems.
11. Assure that project transfer takes place.
12. Maintain communication links across interfaces.

Plan for Integration

Integration doesn't just happen — it must be planned. The project manager must develop a detailed planning document that can be used to get the project initiated, and to assure that all project participants understand their roles and responsibilities in the project organization.

The project manager is the only person in that key position having an overview of the entire system, hopefully from its inception, and can foresee potential interface or other integration problems. After identifying the interfaces the project manager can keep a close surveillance on them to catch and correct any integration problems when they first occur. Particularly important in the project plan is a clear delineation of the project requirements for reporting, hardware delivery, completion of tests, facility construction, and other important milestones.

An important part of the project plan should be the integration plan. This plan may even be a separate document if a single department or even a separate contractor is responsible for project integration. In any case, the integration plan should define and identify all interface problems, interface events, and interrelationships between tasks and hardware subsystems. The integration plan should then analyze the interrelationships between tasks and the scheduled sequence of events in the project.

Develop Integrated Work-Breakdown Structure, Schedule, and Budget

The most important part of a project plan is an integrated work-breakdown structure, schedule, and budget. Whatever type of planning and control technique is used, all the important interfaces and interface events must be identified. Interface events such as hardware or facility completions will be important project milestones. The project network plan must be based on the interface events in order to facilitate analysis of the entire project on an integrated basis. Resource allocation and reporting periods can then be coordinated with interface events, and schedules and budgets can be designed on an integrated basis.

Continually Review and Update Project Plan

The project manager must continually review and update both the administrative and technical portions of the project plan to provide for changes in scope and direction of the project. She or he must assure that budget and resource requirements are continually reviewed and revised so that project resources are utilized in the most effective manner to produce an integrated system.

Assure Project Control and Adherence to Project Plan

The most complete and well integrated project plan is worthless if no one uses it. Only the project manager can assure that all task managers are aware of their role and responsibilities in project success. But continuous follow-up by the project manager is necessary to assure adherence to the project plan, and awareness of any necessary revisions.

Assure Design For An Integrated System

The design step is extremely critical since integration must be designed into the system. Therefore the project manager must exercise considerable influence during the design phase to assure that interfaces are recognized and that the system is designed as an integrated whole. Subsystem designers must work closely with other subsystem designers and the overall system designers to assure complete integration.

Large aerospace projects have often been fortunate enough to afford the luxury of an integrating contractor. This contractor would plan the design and hardware development phases so as to assure effective systems integration. They would prepare an integration plan which would serve as a guide for the other system contractors in designing, developing, testing, and manufacturing the subsystems. The integrating contractor would have responsibility for assembling the overall system. An example would be the development by separate contractors of three separate stages and a warhead by a fourth contractor. A fifth contractor would serve as the systems integrator, guiding the four contractors throughout the development project.

Resolve Conflict Situations

It is inevitable that problems occur at organizational and subsystem interfaces. These problems may or may not result in actual open conflict between individuals or organizations. A common situation is personal conflict between the two managers involved at the interface. Conflict situations result primarily from the concerned groups or managers losing sight of the overall project goals or having differing interpretations of how to get the job accomplished. The project manager must continually be on the lookout for potential and real conflict situations and resolve them immediately.

Remove Roadblocks

Roadblocks are inevitable in a complex organization, and the inevitable result of conflict situations. Resolving the conflict situation will eliminate many roadblocks, but there are always other roadblocks set up intentionally or unintentionally by managers and other personnel not directly involved with the project. These roadblocks may be the result of conflicting needs for resources and personnel, or conflicting priorities for the use of facilities and equipment. Administrative roadblocks often occur because managers outside the project do not understand or sympathize with the project manager's urgency. Such roadblocks are difficult to deal with, and the project manager may be forced to go to top management to get a satisfactory resolution.

Set Priorities

In order to resolve or prevent conflict situations, the project manager is continually faced with the problem of setting priorities. There are two types of priorities that concern the project manager: (1) the overall company or organizational priorities which rate project needs in relation to other projects within the organization, and (2) the priorities within the project for the utilization of personnel, equipment, and facilities. The first type of priority may be beyond the control of the project manager, but it is a problem with which one must be continually concerned. Pity the poor project manager who is so busy getting the job done that he or she forgets to cement relationships with top management. The result may be a low project priority that dooms the project to failure. The second type of priority is within the project organization and therefore within the control of the project manager. These priority problems must be handled on a day-today basis, but in a manner that will promote the integration of the system.

Make Administrative and Technical Decisions Across Interfaces

The project manager must recognize and solve the critical technical and administrative problems and make the critical decisions that arise during the course of a project.

Solve Customer or Client Problems

It is obviously very important to assure that the customer or' client be kept happy. To do this, the project manager must keep the client thoroughly informed both as to the technical status and the schedule/budget status of the project. Top management looks to the project manager as the primary contact with the customer or client, and expects that these relationships be open, honest, and on a friendly basis. The project manager is a very real representative of top management.

Assure That Project Transfer Takes Place

Project transfer is the movement of a project through the project organizations from the conceptual phase to final delivery to the customer. Project transfer does not just happen, it must be carefully planned and provided for in the scheduling and budgeting of the project. The project manager has the responsibility of assuring that project transfer takes place without wasteful effort and on schedule.

The movement of the project from block to block involves crossing organizational interfaces, an action which must be forced if it is to happen on schedule. The basic problem is that of making certain that the project is transferred quickly, without organizational conflict, without unnecessary redesign or rework, and without loss of relevant technology or other information. Experience has shown that the best method of assuring effective project transfer is to utilize people who can move with the project across organizational interfaces. The project manager has two alternatives to facilitate project transfer: (1) the designation of suitably qualified personnel who can move forward with the project, i.e., change their role as indicated by the left to right dashed arrows; or (2) the utilization of personnel who can move backward in the organization and serve as consultants or active working members of the project team. When the project moves forward they serve as transfer agents in moving the project forward in the organization. Various possible personnel transfers are shown by the right to left solid arrows. Great importance must be placed in having customer, manufacturing, and/or construction representatives take part in the design phase.

Maintain Communication Links Across Interfaces

The last of the integration actions, that of constantly maintaining communication links, is perhaps the most difficult and troublesome because it involves the necessity for considerable "people" skill on the part of the project managers. Most project managers find that they spend at least half of their time talking to people getting information, clarifying directives, and resolving conflict and misunderstanding. Much of this time is involved with the critical responsibility for maintaining all communication links both within and outside the project in order to assure project integration. Internal communication links must be maintained between each subdivision of the project, and the project manager must make sure that all the team members talk with each other. In addition, the project manager is personally responsible for maintaining communication linkages outside the project. Many of the external communication links can be personally expedited by the project manager, and in most cases the communication consists of written documents.

Communication linkages internal to the project, however, must function continuously, with or without documentation, and whether the project manager is personally involved or not. These internal communication linkages are most important to the health of the project since they involve the technical integration of the subsystems of the product or project. However, there are usually very real barriers to effective communications across any two such subsystem interfaces. In order to assure that problems do not accumulate and build up at these interfaces, the project manager must act as a transfer agent or a communications expediter.

The project manager must serve as the bridge to make sure that communication barriers do not occur. Communication barriers can be caused by a variety of circumstances and occurrences which the project manager must watch for. A communication barrier may or may not result in actual conflict depending upon the individuals involved.

The project manager is the one person always in a position to expedite communication linkages. He or she can be considered to be a transfer agent by assuring that the communication link is completed by transferring information and project requirements across the interface. Considering the number of interfaces in a complex, multidisciplinary matrix-organized project, this process becomes a major effort for the project manager. The only saving grace is that many of these interfaces will be trouble free with good communications, at least the problems will not all occur at the same time.

Communication barriers may be caused by a variety of circumstances and occurrences. Some of the causes of communication barriers are:

1. Differing perceptions as to the goals and objectives of the overall system will cause problems. Lack of understanding of project objectives is one of the most frequent and troublesome causes of misunderstanding. It can be directly attributed to insufficient action on the part of the project manager, since defining project objectives is a major responsibility. Even when these objectives are clearly stated by the project manager, they may be perceived differently by various project team members.
2. Differing perceptions of the scope and goals of the individual subsystem organizations can likewise restrict communication. Again it is the responsibility of the project manager to clarify these problems, at least as to how they impact the project.
3. Competition for facilities, equipment, materials, manpower, and other resources can not only clog communication routes, but can eventually lead to conflict.
4. Personal antagonisms or actual personality conflicts between managers and/or other personnel will block communications flow. There may also be antagonism toward the project manager by line managers who perceive a threat to their authority or their empire.

5. Resistance to change or the NIH (not invented here) attitude may also detrimentally affect communication links between organizational units.

The project manager has four important communication links: (1) upward to top management, (2) downward to the people working on the project, (3) outward to line managers and other projects at the same level in management, and (4) outward to the customer or client. The project manager has a major responsibility for maintaining communications with the chief executives in the organization. They must be provided with timely, up-to-date progress reports on the technical and financial status of the project. Similar reports must be provided the client or customer, particularly if the customer is outside the company (i.e., the government).

The other important communication link is with the people working on the project. The project manager must keep them informed by means of project directives and personal communications. In addition, there is a continual stream of reports from the discipline/line-organization managers and specialists working on the project. Many of these reports concern details that can be evaluated by administrators and assistant project managers. However, the ultimate decisions as to the worth of the report, and as to whether it should be included in progress reports to the customer and/or top management, is in the hands of the project manager. Communication skills therefore must include the ability to accurately and rapidly evaluate, condense, and act on information from many sources.

Attenuation in these communication links at the organizational interfaces must be minimized. This means that the project manager must have an open line to top management. Conversely too many line managers cannot be interpreting instructions and project goals to the people working on the project. Without open communication links, the project manager will surely fail. There are also a number of important communication links outside the scope of the project, but which may be very important to the health of the project. The project manager has to recognize the existence and the necessity for these communication links.

Rather than fight them, the project manager should endeavor to make use of these relationships.

Summary

Systems integration consists of assuring that the pieces of a project come together at the right time and that it then functions as an integrated unit. However, to accomplish the integration process, all the various types of interfaces must be monitored and controlled, because integration, for the most part, is just another way of saying interface management. In addition, the number of interfaces can increase exponentially as the number of organizational units increase. The life of the project manager can become very complex.

It makes little difference whether "the system" is a missile, a nuclear power plant, a petroleum refinery, or a transportation system, the principles of systems integration are applicable. Similarly, it makes little difference whether the project manager has a pure project organization or is in a matrix organization, the integration function is the same.

A number of positive actions that the project manager must make to assure that integration takes place have been suggested. The most important of these actions is that of maintaining communication links across the organizational interfaces. This once again proves that the principal function of the project manager is to serve as a catalyst to motivate the project team.

9

Managing Project Teams and Assigning Tasks

Introduction

The basic work unit of sports competition, they are the basic work unit of projects. Because of the central role that teams play in projects, it is worthwhile spending some time examining them to gain a better understanding of what they are and to determine how they contribute to project success and failure. With this knowledge, we can then structure project teams to maximize the likelihood that our projects will be carried out effectively.

Characteristics of Project Teams

A team is a collection of individuals who work together to attain a goal. For them to work together, their individual efforts must be coordinated. In sports, coordination is directed by an all-powerful coach and coaching staff. It is achieved through hours of drills and practice sessions. In projects, we have a fundamentally different perspective on teams, since, as we saw in earlier chapters, project managers are rarely all-powerful and the unique and transitory nature of projects does not make them amenable to repetitive drills. Project teams, like projects themselves, come in a great variety of shapes and sizes. Some are large, some small. Some must grapple with highly complex problems, others with routine affairs. Some are highly dynamic, with team members constantly changing, while others are stable.

These last points have interesting implications. In sports teams, a large amount of effort is directed at developing team spirit, which requires team members to have a clear image of what the team is and to identify strongly with it. The presence of team spirit may give a team the competitive edge that allows it to win over equally competent teams lacking team spirit. With project teams, however, team members are often borrowed and may have only the briefest exposure to the project effort. They work on a piece of the project, and when they are done they move on to other projects. Because of this, they may not recognize that they are part of a team. Without such recognition, they are incapable of developing team spirit, or what I have referred to as project commitment.

Of course, from the perspective of the project manager, there *is* a team, whether or not the team members recognize this. The project manager is aware of project goals and knows how the pieces fit together. To the extent that project workers do not realize they are part of a team, however, the project manager's work is more difficult. Clearly, one important task of project managers is the development of some sense of team identification among their staff.

Project teams have structure: there are established rules governing the relationships of team members with each other, with the project manager, with the client, and with the product being developed. How the team is structured will have a strong bearing on a project's prospects for success. A well-structured team can enhance the probability of project success, while a poorly structured team will surely lead to trouble. Good team structure is a necessary, though not sufficient, condition for success; poor team structure is a formula for failure.

One question naturally arises: How can we structure the project team in such a way that it will facilitate the effective management of projects? One answer is to structure the team to enhance team efficiency.

Team Efficiency

In engineering, the concept of efficiency is straightforward. It is defined as the ratio of output to input. If a device consumes 100 energy units of coal (input) and produces 60 equivalent energy units of electricity (output), we say the device is operating at a level of 60 percent efficiency.

We are unable to measure team input and output precisely, so any treatment of team efficiency is necessarily rough. For purposes of discussion, let us loosely define team efficiency as the fraction of potential team performance that is actually achieved. Thus, if a team is accomplishing only a small portion of what it could accomplish under ideal circumstances, its team efficiency is low. If it is achieving as much as is physically possible, its team efficiency is high.

Our concern here is not with how to measure team efficiency precisely but with how to achieve it. How can we structure project teams to enhance team efficiency?

To answer this question, it is useful to understand better why systems are inefficient. Mechanical engineers know that two common and interrelated sources of inefficiency in machinery are machine design and friction. If a machine is poorly designed, it will be inefficient. Poor design often means that the machine is not configured in such a way as to minimize the effects of friction. But even a well-designed machine can operate at less than peak efficiency if, through poor maintenance (for example, improper lubrication), it is subject to the effects of friction.

Team efficiency can be viewed analogously. We can say that a project team can be inefficient because its basic design ensures inefficiency, or because organizational friction keeps it from operating as smoothly as it could or both. Major structural sources of team inefficiency in projects are matrix-based frictions, poor communication, and poor integration of the efforts of team members. The inefficiencies in all three cases are interrelated and are rooted in both design inadequacies and organizational friction.

Matrix-Based Frictions

Projects that are heavily dependent on temporarily borrowed staff that is, projects employing the matrix approach often have built-in inefficiencies. One important cause of inefficiency in a matrix-structured project is lack of staff continuity.

Let's say that Arthur is assigned as a computer programmer/analyst to a project to revamp a hospital's accounts receivable system. He works actively on the project during the early design phase. When the preliminary design is done, he returns to the data processing department, where he is promptly assigned to an office automation project. Two weeks later, top management signs off on the accounts receivable preliminary design and releases funds for a detailed design phase.

Because Arthur is now working on another project, Linda is assigned to the accounts receivable project as the computer programmer/analyst. This is new material for her, so she spends her first week reviewing overall project requirements as well as Arthur's specific contributions. Only after this review period is she ready to work actively on the detailed design phase. When this phase is completed, she returns to the data processing department, where she is immediately assigned to a new project. During the implementation phase of the accounts receivable project, still another programmer/analyst is employed. And so on.

In this kind of situation, which arises commonly in projects, organizational friction is high, with people spending substantial time simply reviewing what others before them have done. Couple this with the lack of project commitment characteristic of high-turnover jobs, and it is evident that team efficiency will be low.

Another important matrix-based source of friction is the project manager's lack of direct control over project staff and material resources. Without direct control, it takes more effort and time to acquire needed human and material resources. Project politics also may enter the picture, so that acquisition of even a simple piece of equipment may trigger a contorted Rube Goldberg chain of events.

Poor Communication

Information is the lifeblood of projects, and communicating this information effectively to the relevant parties is vital to project success. When communication breaks down, the project is in serious trouble.

Of the various kinds of communication-based friction that contribute to team inefficiency, three will be examined here: communication that becomes an end rather than a means, communication channels that suffer from information atherosclerosis, and garbled messages that lead to work being done improperly.

Although this discussion focuses on communication within the project team, communication between the project team and the customers of the product emerging from the project is also very important. If customers' needs are improperly conveyed to the team, the team may produce a deliverable that is rejected and requires rework.

Communication as an End Rather than a Means

As projects become increasingly bureaucratized, proportionately more and more effort is expended on transmitting information and coordinating tasks. On large projects, as much effort may be directed toward communication and coordination as toward carrying out the required tasks.

The number of communication channels can grow quadratically as projects become larger. When a project team consists of two members, there is only one communication channel to maintain. When it consists of three members, there are three channels; four members, six channels; five members, ten channels. In mathematical terms, if the team comprises n members, there are potentially $n\ (n - 1)/2$ channels to be maintained. Thus, even a modest team of 20 members has a possible 190 communication channels.

On most projects, not everyone has a need to communicate with everyone else. Nonetheless, the potential exists to overwhelm projects with communication requirements. When an inordinate amount of time is spent sending and receiving messages, team efficiency is bound to decline.

Information Atherosclerosis

Atherosclerosis is a condition in which arteries become so clogged that blood can barely trickle through them. Information atherosclerosis occurs when communication channels are so clogged that important information has difficulty making its way through them.

The clogging is largely a consequence of requirements that information be processed in a bureaucratically sanctioned fashion. Thus, an important piece of information sent from team member A to team member B may have to pass through five hands before B receives it. Clogging may also be caused by large amounts of useless information floating through channels and blocking the flow of important messages. Here, great effort must be expended to separate useful information from chaff.

The principal consequence of information atherosclerosis is that information flows are retarded, contributing to inefficiencies in the team effort.

Garbled Messages

We are all familiar with the parlor game "Telephone," in which ten or fifteen people sit in a line or a circle while someone whispers a message in the ear of the first person, who whispers it in the ear of the next person, who passes the message to the next individual, and so on. Typically, by the time the message is passed on to the last person, it has undergone some modification.

I introduced myself to the first person, saying, "Hello, I'm David Frame from Donelson House [my dormitory]." After greeting me, he turned to the woman standing beside him and said, "Professor Jones [or whatever her name was], I want to introduce you to Mr. David Frame from Donelson

House." "So nice to meet you," she said. "Are you related to Jim Frame from Schenectady?" I told her I was not, and after a few more seconds of pleasantries, she passed me on to the next official in line, introducing me as Jim Frame from Donelson House. This official chatted with me for a moment and then introduced me to President Lowry as Jim Donelson. Over the next four years, whenever I encountered Dr. Lowry on campus he would smile and say, "How do you do, Mr. Donelson?"

This experience illustrates something that frequently occurs in organizations: messages get garbled. The consequences of garbled messages range from neutral to disastrous. In projects, garbled instructions may lead staff to carry out their tasks incorrectly. If their work has to be redone (assuming the mistake is caught), or if their efforts cause spinoff problems with other tasks, team efficiency drops.

Poor Integration

As we have seen, one of the basic traits of projects is that they are systems, composed of many interrelated pieces. For the system to work, those pieces have to be brought together and fitted into their proper places. This process of bringing things together is called *systems integration*.

Systems integration is an important function of project professionals. They must integrate the pieces of their projects, bringing everything together so that both the project and its product work properly. If integration is not carried out properly, tremendous inefficiencies will be introduced into the project.

Consider, for example, an editor who is compiling a handbook on gardening. The handbook will contain twenty-five chapters, each written by a recognized expert. If the editor does not carefully spell out what she expects of each of the chapter authors if she does not take steps to integrate the pieces into a whole she will have a hodgepodge of chapters turned in to her. Some will be long, some short. Some will be narrated in a folksy manner; others will be rigidly academic in tone. Some will be filled with footnotes; others will lack any references to related material.

Ultimately, if the editor wants a work that hangs together nicely, she will either have to return the chapter manuscripts to the authors, with instructions on how to revise them so that they dovetail with each other, or she and her staff will have to spend enormous amounts of time editing and rewriting the submitted material. In any event, a poor initial effort at integrating the separate chapters into a cohesive book will cause burdensome rework and yield low levels of team efficiency on the project.

This matter of integration is especially crucial in software development projects. In developing complex software, programmers typically work separately on different pieces of the system. Different pieces of equipment that will employ the software may be produced by different vendors, leading to problems of marginal interoperability. Major problems often arise when attempts are later made to integrate the pieces into a whole. What happens, using the jargon of systems analysis, is that "bugs arise at the interfaces." Although the pieces may be internally consistent and bug free, they don't quite fit together, leading the system to malfunction. A great deal of time and effort must be dedicated to trying to get the pieces to fit together. More time is usually spent testing and debugging the system to ensure integration than writing lines of computer code. To the extent that project managers are effective systems integrators, they dramatically increase the efficiency of their project teams.

Structuring Teams

The issue of structuring organizational effort became popular in the 1990s with the promotion of the concept of organizational architecture, which was most fully explicated in a book with that title written by David Nadler and coauthors.

Because we want to structure project teams in such a way that the structure leads to team efficiency, we clearly want to avoid structures that result in the organizational and design frictions just discussed. Thus, a desirable project team structure is one that copes with staff turnover and lack of direct project manager control over resources, enhances effective communication among project team members, and facilitates the integration of the many pieces of the project.

No one structure fits the bill for all projects. A structure that is ideal for one project may fail dismally with another. Various things must be taken into account in configuring a team structure. What is the size of the project? Can staff be permanently assigned to it, or will there be high levels of staff turnover? What is the technical nature of the project? What is the corporate culture like? What are the psychological characteristics of the team members and other relevant project actors?

To illustrate team structure considerations concretely, we will examine the consequences of structuring a hypothetical project in four different ways. The project is a common one faced by professional consultants: to write a technical report on some topic of interest to a client.

Isomorphic Team Structure

The adjective *isomorphic* comes from the Greek *iso*, which means equal or same, and *morph*, which means form or shape. Two things are isomorphic when they share the same structural appearance.

If we configure a project team so that it closely reflects the physical structure of the deliverable the thing that is being produced the team and the deliverable are isomorphic with respect to each other.

With a project structured this way, there is always a real risk that the pieces (the chapters in the example) will not fit together nicely, since each is being developed independently. Clearly, then, a major function of project managers is to serve as integrators. They must interact closely and continually with their staff to make sure that staff members produce pieces that will fit in the final product.

In our example, the project manager should focus on maintaining a consistent writing style among the team members, avoiding duplication among the different chapters, and linking together the material through cross-references between the chapters. One way to accomplish this integration is to hold weekly staff meetings at which team members briefly describe their efforts and compare notes.

There are several advantages to the isomorphic approach. One is that it is organizationally simple. In our example only five communications channels exist out of a potential of fifteen (six players can be connected together in a total of fifteen pairs). Accountability is crystal clear, since each team member is responsible for developing one piece of deliverable. If progress on one chapter of the report begins to lag seriously, the project manager immediately knows whom to talk to in order to find out what the problem is.

Second, if the different modules of the system are independent, the isomorphic approach allows parallel implementation of tasks, which may considerably shorten the amount of time it takes to carry out the project.

Third, this approach is well suited to projects where new staff members are getting their first exposure to a project management environment. Its simplicity eases novices into their new jobs rather than overwhelming them with complexity. Furthermore, the project manager can take on the role of mentor to the new staff, watching over them closely and providing them with important guidance on how projects are carried out in the organization.

In general, the isomorphic approach can be highly effective in dealing with projects on which the different pieces that make up the deliverable are relatively independent of each other. In such cases, problems of systems integration are much smaller than in projects on which the pieces are inextricably tied together.

Specialty Team Structure

A little thought will show that the specialty team structure is simply a variant of matrix management. With this approach, team members are asked to apply their special expertise across a wide array of tasks. Their skills are used where appropriate.

With this approach, project managers face the classic dilemma of matrix management: they have high levels of responsibility (to produce a deliverable), but lack corresponding levels of authority (they do not directly control the borrowed resources who are working on the project).

Another problem is rooted in the unequal distribution of work. Specialist C clearly has her hands full: she is working on half the document's chapters. She presents another problem as well: she is working alone on two of the chapters, so there is a risk that these chapters will not be well integrated into the document.

The specialty team structure nevertheless offers some advantages. For one thing, it requires a fairly high degree of self-management, something that most knowledge workers value. That is, it is primarily up to the team members to determine how they will coordinate their activities. Decision making shifts substantially from the project manager to the team members. Another advantage is that expertise is applied where appropriate.

Egoless Team Structure

Gerald Weinberg noted in *The Psychology of Computer Programming* that a major cause of problems in computer programming projects is the ego of computer programmers. They are often more interested in developing tour-de-force programs than in doing what is necessary to come up with a well-integrated product. Too often, they are not good team players. To deal with this common problem, Weinberg suggested that project teams should be structured to minimize the ill effects of egos. When we look at the product of an egoless team, the results of a truly collaborative effort, it should be difficult to determine who produced what portion of the product.

There is no obvious leader on the egoless team. Decisions are achieved through consensus, and project tasks often reflect the input of all the team members. For example, in the technical report example, team member A may write a draft of the first chapter and then turn it over to team member B, who edits and reworks it. After all the chapters are done, team member C may do a final editing of the report, to make sure that it is well integrated. To the extent that team members collaborate jointly like this, problems of ego will be minimized.

The egoless team structure encourages high levels of interactivity and communication among project members. They are continually in touch with each other and make decisions through consensus. If communication is good and team members are working together toward a common goal, problems of systems integration should be low.

I have heard many scathing criticisms of the egoless team approach by those who have tried to implement it in their organizations. One of the most common is that "the egoless team doesn't work, because people have egos." Project workers, especially those with great talent, possess pride of authorship. They want to make their unique contributions, to stand out from the crowd, and they strongly resist attempts to downplay their egos. Another criticism focuses on the lack of leadership. "Without strong leadership, there is a tendency for egoless teams to drift," comments one project manager who worked in a company that espoused the egoless approach to team structure.

To those who declare that egoless teams go against human nature (and I often hear this comment), I point out that in Asian cultures, with their stress on harmony and consensus, egoless teams are more the rule than the exception. The Western concept of leadership, based on individualism, is alien to the East. Consider the Japanese dictum that states, "The nail that stands up is hammered down."

I believe that egoless teams can work effectively in Western cultures in certain situations. First, team size must be relatively small, since with larger teams, communication channels proliferate, leading to bureaucracy and its attendant inefficiencies. Furthermore, with large teams, it becomes difficult to achieve a meaningful consensus.

Second, egoless teams require continuity in team membership. They are very much like a sports team in this respect. In the 1980s, there was a college basketball team that had four starting players who were brothers. "I spend most of my time trying to get team members used to playing with each other," said the coach. "These brothers have been playing together a whole lifetime. They're remarkable." As with sports teams, team efficiency on egoless teams is highly dependent on the team members' knowing one another's operating styles, technical capabilities, weaknesses, and so on. This knowledge can develop only if staff work together continually. You cannot have egoless teams functioning effectively as a matrix.

Third, egoless teams may function well on ill-defined state-of-the art projects for which the final deliverable is at first only vaguely conceived. Basic research projects typically have these characteristics. A synergistic team (one on which the effectiveness of the combined team is greater than the effectiveness of the individual team members) may be able to pool the talents of the team members and come up with creative solutions that they could not achieve if working alone.

Finally, egoless teams may be effective on projects where highly creative team members resist the imposition of strong leadership, which goes against their grain and which, they feel, restricts creativity.

The egoless team concept is particularly interesting today, because many of its basic tenets have been resurrected in the concept of self managed teams. While self-managed teams possess enormous capacity to tap into the hidden strengths of team members, proponents of this approach should recall some of the lessons learned from our experiences with egoless teams.

Surgical Team Structure

Frederick P. Brooks, in his classic work on managing software projects, *The Mythical Man-Month*, promotes use of an approach he calls the surgical team. (In software project management, this approach, developed originally by Harlan Mills of IBM, is called the chief programmer team concept.) Brooks asks us to consider how a surgical team functions.

At the heart of the team is the surgeon, who performs the surgery on the patient. The surgeon is surrounded by assistants an anesthesiologist, nurses, and interns who provide her with all manner of assistance. In the final analysis, however, it is the surgeon who carries out the surgical procedure. She calls the shots. The primary function of the assistants is to help the surgeon carry out her task most effectively, with *the* surgeon defining effectiveness.

One fundamental objective of the surgical approach in medicine is to allow the surgeon to pursue her work freely, unencumbered by administrative and technical obligations. The surgeon's task is to perform surgery. Billing of the patient can be handled by administrative staff, anesthesia can be administered by an anesthesiologist, surgical tools can be maintained by the nursing staff, examination of removed tissue can be carried out by a pathologist, and so on. Similarly, in project management, one individual is given total responsibility for carrying out the main body of project work while being shielded from administrative paper pushing.

The surgical approach to team structure stands diametrically opposed to the egoless approach. With the surgical approach, all attention focuses on a single individual and his or her abilities. With the egoless approach, it is the overall group effort that counts.

This individual will write the entire technical report. She has been chosen for this position because she writes quickly and clearly and understands the technical content of the study. She is buffered from administrative concerns by a project administrator, who keeps track of hours devoted to the project, progress reports, and the like. She is relieved of editorial burdens by an editorial staff member, who at the end of each day reads her writing, corrects misspellings and grammatical errors, spots and removes minor factual inconsistencies, and so on. In addition, she is provided with technical backup: individuals who are specialists on the material covered in the technical report. If at any point she needs detailed information on a particular topic, she will confer with the appropriate specialist to obtain this information.

At her side is her special assistant, an alter ego who is also a good writer, though perhaps with less experience. The special assistant plays numerous roles. For example, he may serve as an intermediary between the chief writer and the specialists. His most significant role, however, is to keep fully abreast of what the chief writer has done and to take over the project if necessary. The special assistant is an insurance policy against what in project management is called the Mack truck syndrome, which gets its name from the question, "What happens to the project if, on the way to work, the project manager gets hit by a Mack truck?"

A major advantage of the surgical team approach is that it tackles the issue of systems integration head on. Since project output flows from the mind of a single individual, the pieces being produced are likely to fit together nicely. Stylistic and factual inconsistencies and duplication of effort will be minimized. The final product will be well integrated.

One disadvantage of the surgical approach is that it requires a superlatively capable individual to play the role of surgeon. If such an individual is not available, the resulting product may be mediocre.

Another disadvantage is that the surgical team may end up with three bosses. The surgeon is clearly a boss, but principally in regard to technical matters. The project administrator is a boss in the sense that he or she is in charge of maintaining and controlling budgets, schedules, and material resource allocations. Finally, the special assistant may assume responsibility for coordinating and controlling the technical personnel who serve as project specialists. If these three individuals do not communicate with each other clearly and frequently, or if they hold differing perceptions of project goals, team efficiency will be low.

The surgical team approach is most effective on design projects, computer coding projects, and projects that entail large amounts of writing, such as our technical report. Brooks claims that it can also be used effectively on large projects if each project module is given a surgical team structure. When used in this way, according to Brooks, this approach combines small-project efficiency and consistency with large-project scope.

Impact of Team Structure

This discussion of four approaches to structuring a project team is not meant to be exhaustive; many other approaches can be undertaken. Rather, it is illustrative. It shows that for a single project to write a technical report team structure has a dramatic impact on the way in which a project is carried out. It also shows that there is no one perfect structure for management projects. An approach that addresses the issue of systems integration (the surgical team) may lead to confusion as to who is in charge. An approach that fosters intense and open communication among team members (the egoless team) may suffer from lack of leadership. An approach that is conceptually simple and straightforward (the isomorphic team) may yield systems integration problems. And an approach that dovetails nicely in a matrix environment (the specialist team) may have associated with it all the problems that can come with matrix management.

By examining an organization's architecture, project staff develop the ability to predict many of the things that happen on projects, since so much of what happens is structurally induced. Thus, organizational architecture reviews enable project staff to operate proactively. They can anticipate problems and opportunities and work to deal with them early on.

Emerging Structure for Knowledge-Based Projects

Knowledge-based organizations have gradually adopted a project superstructure that is designed to bridge the business-technology gap that many projects encounter. This structure is commonly encountered in the financial sector but can be employed in other sectors as well.

The basic business of financial organizations is engaging in financial transactions. Banks, for example, take deposits from citizens, issue loans to borrowers, offer investments in an array of investment vehicles, make payouts in CDs, and so on. Brokerage firms deal with large volumes of trades of different types of securities. Real estate companies have consortia investing in large development projects. And insurance companies gather premiums from clients and reinvest the money in many ways.

The level of financial transactions in these companies is gargantuan. What makes their businesses viable is heavy use of information technology, specifically computer and telecommunication technologies. Those who carry out projects in the financial sector face an interesting situation of dealing with business in its purest form (the conduct of financial transactions) interacting heavily with technology.

This situation leads to interesting management challenges for people running these projects because the business culture and technology culture are radically different from each other. In business, the principal concern of practitioners is making money. The niceties of process and technique are subservient to the bottom line. Furthermore, the educational background of businesspeople tends to be in the liberal arts and management areas. Most have a limited grasp of technology.

In the technology arena, knowledge and method reign. What you know and your mastery of tools is the key issue. Many technical people have educational backgrounds in computer science, engineering, or the natural sciences. Most of them are committed to designing and implementing optimal technical solutions to problems. Business concerns are secondary.

To deal with the business-technology schism, IT organizations in a wide array of businesses have begun adopting a common approach to managing their software development and maintenance projects. In this approach, key decision making is distributed to a number of significant players in both the business and technology domains rather than put into the hands of a single individual. Like co-managed teams, this structure acknowledges that most projects have a technical and business component to them, so it is designed to serve and integrate these two components.

The specific labels attached to the players may vary from organization to organization, their underlying roles remain constant. The roles of each player will be discussed briefly.

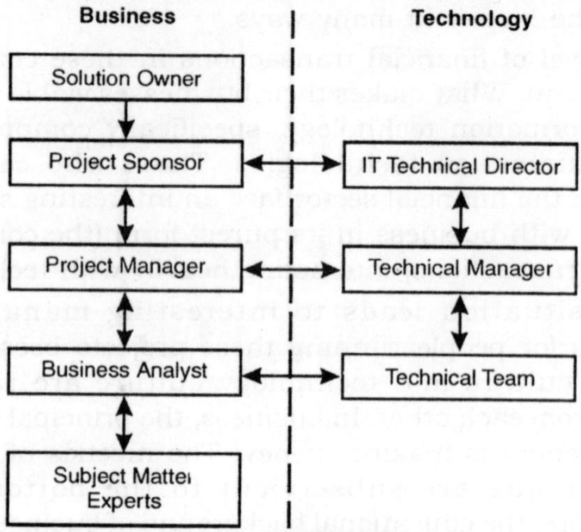

Figure 9.1. Team Structure for Knowledge-Based Projects

Solution Owner

All deliverables have multiple customers, solution owners are in effect the ultimate customer of the deliverable. They are the people who are given primary responsibility for serving customers' interests. On internal projects, they are the senior executives who fund the project. On external projects, they are the most senior executives who have responsibility for making sure that the customer organization receives what it wants.

Project Sponsor

The senior executives who serve as guardian angels of the project within the organization are the project sponsors. By virtue of their senior position, they have power that they can use to support the project effort. For example, if a project team is having difficulty obtaining resources from the design shop, the project sponsor can talk to its head to see if the needed resources can be released quickly. They also serve as the champion of the project in meetings of the organization's most senior executives, to make sure that the project remains visible in the organization.

Project sponsors also play a mentoring role to the project team. Because they are experienced in the ways of the organization, they can offer guidance on what is possible (and not) within the organization. They can also deal with problems arising outside the organization. For example, when the project team has a conflict with a significant customer, they can deal directly with the customer to reduce the level of friction. In this sense, they serve as political godfathers, helping the team to navigate tricky political waters.

Project sponsors also serve the needs of senior management. They keep watch on project developments and make sure that it is achieving goals that meet the organization's requirements. If the project is mismanaged or drifts from its objectives, sponsors can intervene to help set things right.

The importance of project sponsors for enabling project success has been recognized only since the mid-1990s. Prior to that time, projects might have had senior managers helping them out, but this was done on an ad hoc basis for the most part. After that time, sponsors were formally assigned to projects and were given defined roles in the project effort.

In view of the importance of project sponsors to project teams, sponsors must be effective. Often they are not, for the following reason. In many cases, project managers are the ones who recruit sponsors, and they frequently make a common mistake: they try to recruit sponsors from the most senior levels of management on the grounds that these men and women are very powerful. The problem with this approach is that while the executive vice president may agree to serve the sponsor role, it is unlikely that he or she has the time to do a good job. This person may not show up for important meetings, or review significant reports, or champion the team's cause on the executive committee.

After encountering this problem in many organizations, I have established what I call *Frame's Rule for Selecting Sponsors*. The rule goes like this: *Identify the highest-level sponsor that you would like to have to protect the project's interests. Then choose someone one or two layers beneath this individual in the organization's hierarchy.* The rationale for this rule is simple. Having a powerful sponsor on paper is not helpful if the sponsor cannot commit to giving the project's affairs the attention they need. So recruit as a sponsor someone who is both willing and able to help out. If they are close to the high-level executive, they have his ear and can influence support from him when appropriate, so you still can get support from the highest ranks of the organization.

IT Technical Director

The project sponsor is principally a sponsor from the business side of the organization. It is also important to get support from the highest levels of the technical organization to make sure that the project receives the technical resources it needs. If the project team finds that its technical counterparts are not being cooperative, then their project sponsor can approach the IT technical director to see if she can correct the problem. Interestingly, if the technical team members realize that their boss is committed to enabling a project to achieve its goals, they usually function in a cooperative way without prodding.

The project sponsor should work to gain the IT technical director's support for the project, thereby reminding her that the project has strong support from the highest levels of the organization.

Project Manager

With the project team superstructure we are looking at here, project managers play the same role as business managers described in the discussion on the co-management of project teams. Their principal concern is to make sure that business requirements are achieved on time and within budget. A substantial portion of their energy must be devoted to collaborating with their technical counterpart in the IT organization: the technical manager.

Technical Manager

Technical managers play the same role of development managers on co managed teams: they strive to make sure the project achieves its technical requirements on time and within budget. They muster the technical troops to do their jobs as effectively as possible. They devote substantial energy to collaborating with their project manager counterpart.

Business Analysts

The central role of the business analyst is another new development in managing knowledge-based projects. Traditionally, systems analysts had the job of making sense of what customers needed and wanted and wedding these needs and wants to the technology that would be used to satisfy them. They would study the existing system, identify features of the desired system, and take stock of possible technical solutions. Then they would use this information to identify technical requirements, which would be converted into specifications. Though this process, customer needs and wants would be transformed into technical solutions.

Unfortunately, this process led to solutions that were only partially on target: project teams were building deliverables that did not fully address customer needs and wants. Not surprisingly, customers would be unhappy with the outcomes. A big source of problems was that the systems analysts did not understand the business they were dealing with. For example, there might be non accountant systems analysts gathering requirements for an accounting system. Although they might be masters of software design and programming, they didn't know the difference between cash-based and accrual-based accounting.

To deal with this problem, large portions of the systems analyst position slowly evolved over the 1990s into the business analyst role. Unlike systems analysts, who see themselves fundamentally serving a technical function, business analysts have an explicit charge to make sure the customers' business requirements are captured correctly in the technical requirements. Thus, they must know both the business and the technology. In many organizations, business analysts are people who once worked in the technology arena and then migrated to the business side of the enterprise. To make sure they do not forget that their job is to serve the customers, they usually are part of the business team on projects, as indicated in Figure 9.1. Often, they are the key point of liaison between business team members and technology team members.

Subject Matter Experts

The content experts who provide business analysts with the detailed information they need to understand how business processes work are referred to as subject matter experts, or SMEs (pronounced *smeeze*). For example, in developing a comprehensive accounting system, business analysts might draw on the expertise of tax specialists, financial managers, database experts, and general accountants. If the accounting system is going to function over the Web, they would also add Web experts and network specialists to the list of SMEs they need to work with.

Working with SMEs can be challenging. If they are busy doing their regular jobs, they may have trouble freeing up time to help business analysts. Typically, they are experts on the periphery and not major stakeholders in the project, so they may not feel strong commitment to providing insightful responses to the queries of the business analysts. Furthermore, they often have limited knowledge of the technology that is being employed, so they do not know how to phrase their guidance in ways that are meaningful in a technical context. Because of this, business analysts must be trained to communicate effectively with SMEs to help them understand what is needed of them, and then to take the SMEs' lay insights and convert them into technical solutions.

Technical Team

The technical team members are the people who will implement the requirements presented to them by the business analysts. They often have little in-depth knowledge of the business content of the solutions they are working on. Their primary interests are in solving technical challenges with the tools available to them. If these men and women are to develop meaningful technical solutions, their technical director must convince them of their need to commit themselves to meeting project goals and the business analysts must make sure that they understand exactly what needs to be done.

Working Collaboratively

The track record of this project team superstructure has been good. By employing it, we have some assurance that both business and technical issues will be handled effectively. In addition, this superstructure requires businesspeople and technical staff to operate in a collaborative way. Collaboration starts at the top, with the project sponsor and IT technical director agreeing at the outset that they will do what they can to support the project so that it is delivered on time, within budget, and according to specifications and that it ultimately leads to customer delight.

Creating Team Identity

The focus of the discussion thus far has been the mechanical aspects of putting a team together. Beyond mechanics, there is the question of creating a sense of cohesion among the team members. The stumbling block is the familiar problem: people working on projects are typically on loan and have little opportunity or motivation to develop a commitment toward the projects. It is clearly in the interest of project professionals to stimulate a sense of project identity among workers attached to their projects.

There are many ways in which they can do this. What sometimes pulls a team together is the personality and special management style or expertise of the project manager. Charismatic managers or those with a legendary reputation for technical prowess easily catch the attention of their staff, who recognize that they are privileged to work with these managers.

Those who lack exceptional charismatic or technical prowess must work hard at developing a sense of project identity among project staff. Some research I have carried out suggests that team-building efforts on projects should focus on three things: making the team as tangible as possible, building a reward system, and building team spirit by effective use of a personal touch.

Making the Team Tangible

People are not easily motivated by intangibles, so it stands to reason that project professionals should aspire to make their teams as tangible as possible. This is difficult on projects that depend on borrowed resources. Designers are brought in to do their design work. When they are done, they return to their homes in the design shop. The same process is repeated with implementers, testers, sales personnel, purchasing agents, and all the other people who constitute the project team. To these people, the project is largely an abstraction. A survey I conducted of project professionals suggests that they commonly carry out a number of actions to make their teams more tangible. In particular, they use meetings to good advantage, devise a common working space, and give the team a name.

Effective Use of Meetings. The obvious purpose of team meetings is to communicate information. A less obvious function is to establish a concrete team identity. During the meeting, team members get to see that they are not working alone. They are part of a larger group, and the success of the group undertaking depends on the efforts of team members doing their individual parts. One important event that makes the team tangible is the kickoff meeting, when all the project team members assemble at the outset of the project. A number of actions should be carried out at this meeting:

- Players should be identified and a team roster should be distributed.
- A first shot at identifying roles and responsibilities should be made.
- The project charter, which identifies the rationale for the project, should be distributed, with key milestones highlighted.
- If possible, a high-level manager should be present to demonstrate top management's commitment to the project effort. If the project has a project sponsor, his or her presence is absolutely vital.

Another important meeting is the status review. Status reviews are periodic meetings (say, biweekly) to examine project performance. These reviews offer team members a chance to get together and reaffirm their commitment to serving the interests of the larger group.

Meetings need not be formal. Beer and pretzel parties, team softball games, and other social activities are meetings of sorts. Just as with more formal meetings, they enable team members to develop a palpable sense of team identity.

Colocation of Team Members, War Rooms, and Web Sites. The most obvious way to make the team tangible is to have team members work together in a common space. The problems with this approach are practical: Who has the space to collect team members? Does it make sense to locate people physically in the team space if they are going to be on the job for only a couple of days?

An effective substitute for collection is the creation of a war room. The war room can be as elaborate as the high-tech electronics-filled rooms serving the defense community or as humble as a converted closet. War rooms contain the most significant project documentation. Frequently, their walls are covered with PERT/CPM charts, cost charts, and the other appurtenances of project planning and control. Their primary significance from the perspective of this discussion is that they serve as a tangible sign of the project effort. Even when they are far removed from the core team activities, project personnel can associate their rather abstract team with its physical embodiment, the war room.

Today, war rooms are increasingly being replaced by project Web sites. It is a rare project today that lacks a Web site, which is really a virtual war room. Team members can access the site twenty-four hours a day, seven days a week, to determine whatever information they need about the project. A good Web site provides information on schedule status and job assignments and contains the minutes of status meetings. Through the Web site, team members can access important documentation, such as the project charter and the statement of work.

Creation of a Team Name. The creation of a team name is a common device for making the project team more tangible. Frequently, an associated team logo is also created. The name and logo might be affixed to such things as stationery, T-shirts, coffee mugs, and caps. If done with good humor, this collection of "trinkets and trash" (as project staff have dubbed them) can serve a significant role in developing team identity.

Building a Reward System

So long as project professionals lack the carrots and sticks needed to catch people's attention, it is difficult for them to motivate project team members. Lacking the standard corporate rewards and punishments, they must invent their own reward systems. Here are some suggestions from the creative project professional's bag of rewards:

Letters of commendation. Although project professionals may not have responsibility for their team members' performance appraisals, they can write letters commending their project performance. These letters can be sent to the workers' supervisors, to be placed in their personnel files.

Public recognition for good work. Superlative workers should be publicly recognized for their efforts, and not just at the end of the project but on various occasions. For example, it might be a good practice to begin each status review meeting with a brief mention of project workers who have exceeded their project goals.

Job assignments. Project professionals should recognize that although they may not have much budgetary authority, they have substantial control over how the team members spend their time. They should recognize that job assignments can be used to reward and punish team members. Good work should be rewarded with challenging job assignments.

Flexible work time. Good project workers who need adjustments in their working hours might be rewarded with some measure of flexibility. Workers who have put in many hours of overtime might be given an occasional day off as a reward.

Job-related perquisites. Most work environments have special features that can serve as motivational perquisites. Common examples of perks include a convenient parking space, access to a company car, nice office space, and use of a cellular phone. Such perks should be offered to the best workers.

New equipment. Whenever new equipment is to be allocated among project workers, the first pieces should be distributed to the best workers as a clear sign of appreciation for their efforts. This is a particularly useful motivational approach when dealing with technical people, who take great interest in their tools.

Recommendation for cash awards or bonuses. Many organizations have established cash awards for their best performers. Project professionals can use these awards as an incentive to do good project work.

Using a Personal Touch

The third general means by which project professionals can build a sense of team identity is the effective use of the personal touch, the one-on-one relationship between project professionals and their borrowed staff. When managers establish a personal rapport with their team members, they create an environment where the team members are willing to walk the extra mile to achieve project goals. The list of things managers can do to strengthen their personal touch can go on for pages. Following is a short list of actions that have been particularly effective in building team spirit on projects:

Be supportive. Team members appreciate a supportive manager. There are various ways in which managers can support their teams. Physical support may be achieved by doing everything possible to make the work environment pleasant. Psychological support may be reflected in such actions as defending project workers against attack by outsiders and expressing appreciation for the efforts of the project team.

Be clear. One of the most common complaints that employees express about their managers is unclear expectations, muddled instructions, and lack of meaningful feedback. Team members appreciate working in an environment where clarity dominates and confusion is minimized.

Learn something about the team members. Many effective project professionals go to great lengths to learn as much as possible about their team members, including their personal interests, information about their family, and their accomplishments.

Celebrate special occasions. Project professionals can further demonstrate their interest in their team members by celebrating the occurrence of special occasions of importance to the workers for example, birthdays, anniversaries with the organization, and special achievements.

Be accessible. Project managers will not build much team spirit if they are perceived as cool and distant. They should be accessible, enlisting an open-door policy. They should encourage team members to offer their views on project-related issues.

Summary

Projects are carried out through teams, but these teams are typically fragmented and poorly defined owing to the exigencies of matrix management. An important function of project managers is to consciously create a team structure where no discernible structure exists. This is not a trivial matter, since there are countless ways teams can be organized. One prime consideration in structuring a team should be to select a structure that contributes to team efficiency.

It is not enough simply to select an appropriate team structure, however. Team members must be encouraged to identify with the team, develop team spirit, and do whatever is necessary to make the project succeed. The problem is that team members are usually on temporary loan to the project and have little stake in whether it succeeds or fails. Project managers must create a sense of identity in an environment that does little to encourage a cohesiveness and make stakeholders out of their staff. They can do this through a number of ways, particularly by making the team as tangible as possible, creating a reward system to reward good behavior, and displaying a caring personal touch in their dealings with team members.

10

ACHIEVING RESULTS FOR SUCCESS OF PROJECT

Introduction

When things are popping all around them, it is difficult for them to step back and view their projects from a distance. We do precisely that: stand back and take a big picture view of the project management process as it pertains to information age projects. What are the elements of good project management the most rudimentary principles that we should keep in mind to maximize the likelihood that we will bring our project to a successful conclusion?

Rudimentary Principles

There are five basic principles that, if followed, will help project professionals immeasurably in their efforts:

1. *Be conscious of what you are doing; don't be an accidental manager.* Project management, as we have seen, has been called the accidental profession. Men and women stumble into project management responsibilities accidentally, only vaguely aware of what projects are and how they should be managed. Their management approach is pure trial and error. They reinvent the wheel, and in most cases do a bad

job of it. The pity is that much of the grief they encounter and much of the waste they engender could be avoided if they made an effort to learn something about the theory and practice of project management. For example, if they learned that project staff are usually borrowed workers over whom they seldom have any direct control, they could direct their energies toward *influencing* these workers to do well rather than spend time sulking in a corner because of what they perceive as the insubordination and lack of commitment of these people.

In order to maintain consciousness of the fact that they are working on something over which they have the power to do a good job *if only they knew what they were doing* perhaps project professionals should say to themselves several times a day, "I am a project professional. I work on projects. Projects are undertakings that are goal oriented, complex, finite, and unique. They pass through a life cycle, which begins with project selection and ends with project termination." The purpose of this ritualistic litany is simply to remind the project professional that over the past several decades, many people have thought a lot about what projects are and what their management entails. Projects are hard to manage even when we know what we are doing. They are nearly impossible to manage by accident and happenstance.

2. *Invest heavily in the front-end spadework; get it right the first time.* Many of us have a tendency to rush in where angels fear to tread. We tend to leap before we look. We are results oriented and often overlook some rudimentary matters regarding the basic steps it takes to achieve these results. This characteristic serves some people well: by throwing caution to the wind, they achieve breakthroughs that more cautious people would never accomplish. Such people are trailblazers—bold, dynamic, and filled with exuberant energy.

This tendency to leap before we look also has its drawbacks. Where, for example, does one draw the line separating boldness from impetuosity? Fearlessness from foolishness? In many situations, a moment's reflection on what action to pursue is more important than boldness. For the most part, projects can use more forethought and less impetuosity.

By definition, projects are unique, goal-oriented systems; consequently, they are complex and cannot be managed effectively in an offhand, ad hoc fashion. They must be carefully selected and carefully planned. A good deal of thought must be directed at determining how they should be structured. Great amounts of time must be spent hand holding with customers (internal or external) to ensure that the final deliverable is something they find useful.

Care taken at the outset of a project to do things right will generally pay for itself handsomely. Doing things right takes time and effort. For example, it takes time to find out what the real needs are on a project, specify requirements carefully, and plan out a course of action for accomplishing project objectives. For impetuous people, it is far more satisfying to rush into projects and begin solving problems than to identify precisely what those problems are.

Unfortunately, if the proper spadework is not done at the outset of a project, it is likely that various project tasks will not be done properly; those tasks will have to be redone again and again until project staff finally get them right. Rework is expensive. It is invariably more expensive to rework something than to take the time to do it right at the outset.

3. *Anticipate the problems that will inevitably arise.* This book has stressed repeatedly that many of the problems that project professionals face are predictable. For example, if project professionals are working in a matrix organization, we know that they will face the following people problems:

- They will have little or no direct control over the borrowed staff members.
- Their staff will have little commitment to the project.
- Their staff are not likely to be precisely the workers they want or need.

We can also count on the following additional realities:

- The goals of portfolio managers are often different from those of individual project managers, since maximization of portfolio performance will likely require suboptimization of the performance of individual projects.

- Schedule and budget variances will occur, since it is impossible to predict the future precisely. We should not ask, "Do we have variances?" but rather, "Are the variances we face acceptable?"
- Customer needs will shift.
- If project requirements are stated vaguely, they are likely to be misinterpreted. (They may also be misinterpreted even when they are stated precisely.)
- Over planning and over control will lead to project inefficiencies and may result in cost and schedule overruns, just as with under planning and weak control.
- All projects have hidden agendas, which are usually more important than the stated agenda.

By reviewing these inevitable realities (and this is only a small sampling from a much larger list), we see that conflict and problems are built into projects and will arise. If we anticipate these problems, however, we can determine in advance how to cope with them. As we become more experienced project managers, we can even learn how to use them to our advantage.

Go beneath surface illusions; dig deeply to find the real situation. Project managers are continually getting into trouble because they accept things at face value. For example, customers usually have only the vaguest conception of what their needs are, even when they think they know exactly what they want. The project manager who blindly accepts a customer's needs statement is likely to encounter customer requests later for major changes in the project, or perhaps that manager will produce a deliverable that the customer rejects, saying, "This is neither what we asked for nor what we want."

As another example, a project manager, assuming that secretaries are *the* customer of a project to install a new document management system in the office, fails to determine the needs of such hidden customers as the secretaries' bosses, the office's clients, and the division's information resource manager. Consequently, while secretaries' needs are met, the needs of the other significant actors may be unsatisfied, possibly resulting in project failure.

To the extent that project professionals do not understand what is really happening on their projects, they are likely to be chasing after shadows. They will not make the right decisions.

Robert Block's approach to project politics, described in *The Politics of Projects*, can greatly help project managers to be more realistic. Using his approach, they systematically go through a number of steps designed to let them penetrate surface illusions and identify what is really happening. First, they identify all the players, paying special attention to those who can have an impact on the project outcome. Then they try to determine the goals of the players and the organization, focusing particularly on hidden goals. Having done this, they assess their own strengths and weaknesses. It is only at this point that they should begin defining the problems facing them in their project.

It is crucial to the problem definition step that project managers root their efforts in reality isolating the facts, identifying the real situation, and recognizing the assumptions underlying the whole project effort. Once the problem is defined adequately, they can develop solutions, test them, and fine-tune them.

5. *Be as flexible as possible; don't get sucked into unnecessary rigidity and formality.* Project management can be viewed as a struggle to contend with the basic principle of the second law of thermodynamics, which states that things tend to dissolve into a state of random disorder. With project management, we try to reverse this sequence, creating order where the natural state seems to be chaos.

In our drive to create order, however, we run the risk of sacrificing reasonable flexibility on the altar of formal project requirements. The rationale for inflexibility is that order comes from structure: we convince ourselves that the more formal the structure is that we impose on projects, the less chaos we face. Thus, we may require all project changes to be approved by three levels of management, and we may require staff to fill out six-page progress reports every week.

We may also put together very detailed plans for the project, so that nothing is left to chance. We may hold daily staff meetings to make sure that workers know what they are supposed to do. And so on. In this attempt to realize order, we may instead achieve stifling bureaucracy.

One of the hardest tasks facing policymakers in project organizations is striking a balance between the need for order and the contrary need for flexibility. Why is flexibility necessary? Because projects are full of surprises, and overly rigid systems cannot respond adequately to surprises, just as a rigid stick will snap after it has been bent only a little. This is especially true with information age projects, which deal with intangibles and tend to be amorphous. By their very nature, they are hard to plan in detail and defy attempts at tight controls.

Too often people do not understand that order can be attained without excessive formality. If we are conscious of what we are doing on projects and avoid being accidental project managers, invest in front-end spadework, anticipate inevitable problems, and penetrate beneath surface illusions, we will help establish order in our projects. If, in addition, we reject unnecessary formality and rigidity, we may be able to have our cake and eat it too that is, we may be able to achieve order and flexibility simultaneously.

Strong degrees of formality are appropriate on some projects. For example, as projects get larger, the number of communication channels that must be maintained grows explosively, and formal protocols must be established to coordinate communication efforts. As a consequence, it is common in programs with budgets greater than $100 million to find from 50 to 65 percent of the total project budget dedicated to project administration.

Heavy formality may also be appropriate on low-risk projects when we know precisely what must be done to produce the desired deliverable. When we build a house in a development of nearly identical houses, for example, we specify in detail many formal requirements that project staff should meet; we leave nothing to chance. Such low-risk projects have a minimal need for flexibility, since they encounter fewer surprises than high-risk projects.

Information age projects typically do not fall into either of these two categories. First, because they deal with information rather than with bricks and mortar, they do not usually achieve the size of projects to construct buildings or build fighter aircraft. Second, because they deal with intangibles and are hard to get a handle on, they tend to be filled with uncertainty. Given the smaller size of typical information age projects and their high degree of uncertainty, the need for rigid formality in their management is generally low; therefore, in most such cases, heavy formality is undesirable. Nevertheless, this call for flexibility on information age projects should not be used as an excuse for poor planning and control.

I believe that the project management environment is more akin to the environment of the trouble spot than of Scotland. Wandering through project management terrain can be dangerous to the naive. In the land of project management, things can and will go awry.

It is also true that being a project manager can be an enormously rewarding experience. For many individuals, managing projects is their first foray into management. It allows them to develop the management skills they need for career advancement. In addition, it offers them an independence of action and a degree of responsibility they infrequently encounter in other areas. For people who thrive on challenges, like to solve problems creatively, and enjoy creating order out of chaos, the management of projects can be exhilarating.

11

Organizational Support for Project Management

Introduction

Many project managers didn't choose project management as a career; they had the job thrust upon them. And in some cases, this is because the organization has no separate career path for project managers and technical people. If you want to advance in your career as a technical person, you do so by becoming a project manager.

The result is often tragic. You lose a good technical person over time because it is almost impossible to maintain a high level of technical skills and also be a manager. And you also find that many of these technical specialists make poor project managers because they lack the people skills that are so vital to doing the job well.

The first thing you should consider is that selecting people who have the desire and aptitude for the job is critical to the ultimate success of that individual in the job. Just because a person is good at his or her technical job does not mean that he or she will make a good project manager. In fact, if she is exceptionally good at technical work, she will probably *not* make a good project manager, one reason being she will find it hard to manage the project without meddling in the technical work.

The message is: If you select for the job a person who is unsuited for it, you will just have to replace that individual later on, so you have done him or her a great disservice in placing him in the job.

As we have tried to show, not everyone is cut out to be a project manager, any more than everyone is cut out to be a butcher, baker, or candlestick maker. To each of us is given certain aptitudes, and rather than try to force the square peg into a round hole, it is far better to find a round peg in the first place.

We have shown the kind of attributes that make good project managers. Use these as guidelines in selecting people for the job. Then go the next step and give them the support they need to really make it.

Support the Developing Project Manager

Aptitude is the starting point, but aptitude must be turned into skill. We can learn a good lesson from sports. A coach finds a person who seems to have a real aptitude for a sport. Does the coach put the player on the team and say, "Go play ball?" No. He nurtures the natural talent of the rookie. He teaches him how to use his skills to advantage, to get progressively better. By the time a player becomes a star, his former coaches have invested an enormous amount of time in nurturing that talent, training, practicing, rehearsing. Nobody is *born* a superstar.

We seem to be totally unaware of this in organizations. We use the *shark-bait* approach to dealing with people in the work place. We throw a person into a job with no concern for whether they have aptitude, then give them no help, let the sharks eat them up, then fire them when they don't perform.

We talk about human resource *development*, but seldom is true HRD applied to anyone other than rising superstars who are on a fast track to the top of the organization. We need to do the same for other members of the enterprise especially project managers.

Encourage fledgling project managers to treat their job as a true career path, not as an accidental job. Suggest that they join the Project Management Institute and attend regular chapter meetings so they can network with other members of the profession. Assign a mentor to help guide them. Encourage them to hang in there when the going gets rough, because it will get rough on some projects.

Start them with small jobs and gradually increase their responsibilities until they can handle the really big jobs.

Above all, make sure they get the training they need in the project management body of knowledge, which we have discussed in an earlier chapter of this book. One way to do this is to enroll them in certificate programs offered by universities and other providers around the country. Have them become project management professionals (PMP®). Or, if the person is really serious and excited about project management as a profession, encourage him or her to get a master's degree in project management. This is equivalent to an MBA, but with project management as the primary focus.

Position Itself

Another thing that is important is to give the position some standing in the organization. For a very long time, functional managers have been "king," and project management has been a stepchild that many of those managers resented. In their book *Creating an Environment for Successful Projects*, Robert J. Graham and Randall L. Englund suggest that organizations should view functional groups as being there to serve the needs of projects. In doing so, project managers are elevated to the same status in the enterprise as that of functional managers, if not slightly higher. Only in this manner can project managers get the level of support from functions that they really need to meet critical project targets.

The position of project manager should also have the standing of other positions by giving it a proper job description, pay scale, and so on. Further, the organization should establish a true dual career path, in which technical personnel can advance up a technical ladder and make as much money as members of the management staff. By doing this, they are less tempted to become managers when their true love is technical work. In addition, those individuals who really want to manage projects can do so and hone their skills to perfection.

Actually, there is good reason to suggest that perhaps the ladder should have three branches rather than two. There is definitely a difference between managing projects and managing a department. Since the project manager frequently has people assigned to her team by functional managers, so that she has a lot of responsibility and no authority, she needs a slightly different set of skills compared with those of the department manager. She has to worry less about performance appraisals and daily administrative duties, but she has to have exceptional political skills something that is not quite as critical to the functional manager.

We believe, in fact, that the role of project manager will eventually become the stepping-stone for high-level CEOs, because project managers usually have to interact with people from nearly every department in the organization, as well as people outside. We also believe that, like CEOs, the project manager who has a balanced HBDI profile will have the advantage of being able to interface with people who have any and all thinking preferences, because she can communicate well with them and translate between the different quadrants.

This should not be misunderstood, however. We are not suggesting that *only* individuals with balanced profiles be selected as project managers. For one thing, only about 2 percent of the population have such profiles, so you won't find many candidates who match the requirement. But most importantly, we have shown that people of all profiles can be good project managers if they are willing to augment their least-preferred thinking styles with extra effort or support from team members who have those preferences.

Project Office

To some managers, the term "project office" conveys the idea of bureaucracy and attendant red tape. So if you don't like this term, call it a "project management function," because that is what it is, and we believe from our experience that there is great merit in organizing this way. As we have shown, not everyone is cut out to be a project manager, so having a function staffed by dedicated project managers has a number of advantages. Some of these are discussed as follows:

The project manager can hone his or her skills because that is the entire function to be performed. He or she can develop both breadth and depth in project management skills. She is freed from the temptation to do both managing and doing. Her role is to manage the project, not to do technical work. This frees the technical people from the "burden" of doing project administrative work, which many of them hate doing, and allows them to develop their technical competencies in the same way that project managers develop theirs.

Ultimately, the project office should employ a full-time scheduler if there are four or more project managers. This person can be a clerical level person, who can free project managers to do management rather than sit in front of a computer several days a week massaging their schedules. We have worked with several companies that have done this and realized significant cost savings. A fringe benefit is that the clerical person gets to do something more challenging than routine clerical duties. This truly puts the project manager on an equal footing with other functional managers, since the project office is now viewed as a function in its own right.

The office serves as the focal point for the entire organization. It is now easier to achieve alignment of projects with overall enterprise strategy, because fewer project managers can become more closely aligned with that strategy than is possible when everyone is trying to manage projects. Does this setup mean that other members of the organization need know nothing about project management? Not at all. One of the core principles of good project management is that the people who must do project work should participate in developing the project plan. So everyone needs some understanding of project management.

It displays a typical organizational structure and placement of a project support office. We include it here because it will be instructive to identify the players and how they can be of help to you in your professional development.

Let's take a closer look at who those players are and how they can be of help. Let's start at the top. Business relationship managers are the link between the project support office and the business units. Each business unit will have at least one such person, and they will have firsthand knowledge of all the projects that are planned for their business unit. Find out what those projects entail and whether any of them offer you development opportunities. If so, you will want to take a personal interest in following them along the path to approval and putting in your bid to get on those project teams. The next player of interest to you will be the project support office manager. They should have an enterprise-wide perspective on projects that are nearing the proposal stage or that have staffing needs. While this is a little further along in the project life cycle than the knowledge that a business relationship manager will have, they are still valuable to you for exactly the same reasons as the business relationship manager. You need to be on the inside with all of these people. The other two positions of interest will be the current project managers and the resource managers. And so you can see how the project support office offers a number of opportunities.

Executive Briefings

This raises an important issue. We find many enterprises that spend significant amounts of money training people in project management without realizing the expected gains from their investment. The reason is that middle and senior managers do not understand what project management is.

The common misconception is that project management is just scheduling. Jim Lewis even found this in Germany. A manager in a German company told him that he was trying to explain to senior managers what project management is, and one of them said, "I don't understand why we don't just buy Microsoft Project and do it [meaning project management]." Jim assured him that this same belief is alive and well in the United States.

The reason for this is simple: Until recent years, business schools did not deal with project management. It was not recognized as a specialized discipline, so many senior managers have had no formal education in what it is all about, and they have unrealistic expectations about what project managers can achieve.

As an example of this, a fellow who attended Jim's class on project management told him that when he returned to work, he got his team into the conference room and started developing a plan for his project. His boss came by, saw them in the meeting, and called the project manager outside. "What are you doing?" he asked.

"Developing a project plan," said the project manager. "You don't have time for that," snapped his boss. "Get them out of the conference room so they can get the job done."

And this attitude is more prevalent than you may think. To a great extent, we pay lip service to planning, but most of us don't "walk the talk." This leaves would-be project managers feeling frustrated and unappreciated. More importantly, they are paralyzed and ineffective as a result.

If, as Tom Peters contends, project management is a core competency without which organizations cannot survive in this new millennium, then we need to develop a better understanding and appreciation for what it is all about and support it in the same way that we would support any core competency.

Further, as we have mentioned, projects must be aligned with business strategy. This is commonly referred to as project portfolio management. The enterprise has a portfolio of projects that are key to its overall business strategy. These have been carefully selected and are managed by project managers who have the skills needed for success.

Change your Accounting Procedures

Organizations that have not had strong project management typically budget only departments, and projects are just accidental to how they do work. This is unacceptable if you want to really manage projects correctly.

A project must have its own budget. It is indeed a paper transfer within the organization when the project is strictly internal, but it is a major element of proper project control. What we are saying is that people from functional groups who are assigned to the project have their time charged to the project, which goes back to their departments as a budget credit. This is one way to make everyone aware of what a project really costs, and keeps functional managers from jealously guarding the time of their people because they don't want to spend money from their own budgets unwisely.

You also must have a proper project information system, which means that time spent on the project is charged to the job, not to the functional department, and the same for other expenses.

- You should have a project review board that is responsible for approving changes to project plans.
- You must have a proper project selection process, so that projects don't just ooze up out of the mud without having business merit.
- You should also have a project cancellation process that kills projects that have become losers.

You must allow project managers to have input to the performance appraisals of team members. They would not appraise the technical performance of those people, but rather evaluate such factors as cooperativeness, communication, timeliness of work, commitment to the project, and so on. Only by having such input can a project manager hope to have commitment and loyalty to the project.

Changing the Organizational Culture

When you have been running projects for years in a totally unstructured way and you decide to adopt a structured approach, this is a major change in culture. Any senior manager who has ever tried to change the organization's culture knows that it is not easy. People who are SJ temperaments are motivated to maintain stability and order, and these individuals often occupy many of the middle management positions in any company. So the very change that the senior executive wants to make may be unconsciously resisted by the very people who must help make it happen.

Experience has shown that it takes from two to five years for an organization to reach maturity in project management. There are about five levels of maturity, and it often takes a year per stage.

Dr. Harold Kerzner wrote a book entitled *In Search of Excellence in Project Management*, in which he reported his findings in a survey of approximately 250 organizations, out of which only thirty-nine met his criteria for excellence in project management. No doubt if he had been able to survey the thousands of organizations nationwide that are trying to make project management work, he would have found a much smaller percentage of excellent organizations.

Knowing that it takes time to achieve results is helpful, because when we engage in some change effort, thinking we will achieve quick results, and find that this is not happening, it is easy to lose patience and give up the effort. This is part of what happened with the quality circle movement, the self-directed work team movement, and other programs that promised great rewards. The companies that stayed with these programs usually got results, but many other organizations abandoned them after a brief foray, because results were not quickly forthcoming.

There has been much written about organizational change, and one premise is that a "burning platform" issue is needed to provoke such change and make it "take." The term comes from an incident that happened on a North Sea oil platform. They had a fire, and one individual jumped several hundred feet into the frigid water of the North Sea. The prevailing wisdom is that you can only survive in that temperature for about fifteen minutes, so jumping in is not usually the best thing to do.

When asked why he had jumped, anyway, the man said, "It was certain I would be fried if I stayed on the platform. I figured I may as well take my chances in the water."

Unless the platform is burning and there is no other hope for survival, they won't engage in the real change that is needed. They will try various patches, which usually only attack symptoms, while leaving underlying problems unsolved.

If your organization is experiencing a burning platform issue, you can expect that many people are ready for change and may well embrace it. But do you have to wait until the situation is so critical to initiate change?

Not according to John McDonald. He says there are two kinds of responses to our environment that organizations can make. One is revolutionary change, which is typified by the burning platform. The other is evolutionary change, in which everyone recognizes that the situation is not critical but that it will become so if change is not made. It is usually much less costly, less traumatic, and much smoother to engage in evolutionary change, so we would urge senior managers to try to initiate this kind of change program rather than wait until the platform is on fire.

Change the Reward System

There is a tenet of organizations that says, "What is rewarded gets done." Everyone is inclined to maximize those measures that are used to assess their performance and that may be used to dispense rewards. For example, you cannot reward competition and expect cooperation. You cannot measure functional managers on how well their departments perform and expect them to willingly give resources to projects when doing so will hurt their department performance.

What behavior do we want to encourage?

Ask yourself: what behavior do we want to encourage? Then set up reward systems that will get the desired result. And be careful of concluding that you must have incentive pay systems in place. The most powerful rewards are intangibles—a pat on the back from one's boss, recognition and admiration from one's peers, and the fun and challenge of doing the work itself. Consider these and how they currently work, and make whatever changes are needed to get the results you want.

Walk the Talk

One given is that good projects require teamwork, and teamwork means that people work in a cooperative manner. If the senior management team does not work as a team, if they engage in political backstabbing, then employees at lower levels will not work as teams, either. You have to walk the talk. Lead by example. So you must begin with yourselves, make necessary changes, and then you can ask for those changes in others.

Conclusion

You can't just train project managers and expect that project management will become a way of life next week. Nor can you buy everyone a copy of a scheduling software package and hope that it will make instant project managers of them. There is no instant pudding recipe for making project management work. It takes hard work, and must be both supported and driven by senior management.

12

Specifying Aims and Goals of Project

Introduction

Projects are filled with similar misunderstandings between customers and project staff. What customers order—or, more accurately, what they *think* they order—is often not what they get. Consider the following conversation between an office worker and a painter contracted to paint his office:

OFFICE WORKER: Not only did you paint my office walls blue, but you painted the ceiling blue as well.

PAINTER: You asked me to paint the room blue, and now you've got a blue room.

OFFICE WORKER: But the blue ceiling is oppressive. Ceilings should never be the same color as the walls. They should always be a lighter color.

PAINTER: You asked for a blue room. You're lucky I didn't paint the floor blue as well.

This conversation captures in a nutshell the essence of a major source of misunderstandings on projects: the inadequate statement of customer requirements. The office worker's description of how he wanted the room painted meant one thing to him and another to the painter. As a consequence, the room was not painted to the office worker's satisfaction. Had his requirements been more carefully stipulated, he probably would have gotten what he wanted.

The blame for the poor specification of requirements does not rest entirely on his shoulders. The painter must share some culpability. It was clearly in her interest to make sure she understood exactly what the office worker wanted. As a professional painter, she should devise an approach to dealing with clients that allows her to determine precisely what their requirements are. For example, before beginning each paint job, she might give the client a checklist asking what colors the walls should be, the ceilings, and the trim. Otherwise, clients will continue to be unhappy when she does not do what they want, and they will see to it that she is unhappy as well.

One major objective of those who are effective in designing and implementing projects is to reduce such misunderstandings to a minimum. This can be done with the careful specification of customer requirements.

Nature of Requirements

Requirements specify what the project deliverable should look like and what it should do. They can be divided into two basic categories. *Functional requirements* describe the characteristics of the deliverable in ordinary, non technical language. They should be understandable to the customers, and the customers should play a major, direct role in their development. *Technical requirements* describe the features of the deliverable (for example, its physical dimensions and performance specifications) in detailed technical terms. These technical specifications offer project staff crucial guidance on what they should be doing on the project. Because of their technical nature, technical requirements are unlikely to be understood by the customers. In this chapter, most of our attention will focus on functional requirements.

Project requirements are important for at least two reasons. First, they are a tangible embodiment of the customers' needs. Needs emerge, are recognized and carefully articulated, and then are translated into requirements, which serve as the basis of the project plan. In the final analysis, project planning reduces to the effort of determining how best to meet requirements. If they are specified wrongly or even poorly, the plan will be inadequate.

Second, requirements are important because they define the project team's obligations to the customers. Carefully specified project requirements detail the team's responsibilities. On projects run under contract, the specified requirements are written as a statement of work, and compliance or noncompliance with the contract is determined by resolving whether the contractor has fulfilled the statement of work.

Problems with Requirements

Requirements-related problems are one of the principal sources of cost and schedule overruns. They may lead to rejection of the deliverable or to major reworking of project tasks. Furthermore, they contribute substantially to what I perceive to be the most serious category of project failure: the production of a deliverable that is never used or is misused. Requirements-related problems result in several ways: the requirements that are specified are incorrect, they are imprecise and ambiguous, or they shift as the project is carried out.

Regardless of the specific nature of the requirements-related problem, its consequences unfold with consistent regularity. Here is what happens. During the course of the project, the customers become aware that what the project staff are developing is not what they want. This may reflect the fact that the project staff are working on something completely at variance with what the customers want (incorrect requirements), or they have misinterpreted the customers' stated desires (imprecise, ambiguous requirements), or the customers have changed their minds about what the project staff should develop (shifting requirements). Whichever problem it is, the customers and the project staff are out of sync, and the flow of the project is interrupted.

If the project staff respond to the customers' concerns and do what the customers want and they should if they have grossly misconstrued the desires of the customers the project will have to be replanned, delays will occur, and cost overruns are likely. If they do not act in accordance with the customers' desires, the project's deliverable is not likely to be very meaningful to the customers, suggesting that the project was a waste of time and resources.

Project professionals are faced with a no-win situation here. When requirements-related problems arise, those working on the project encounter either the likely prospect of cost and schedule overruns or strong customer dissatisfaction. Their best bet is to avoid this problem before it surfaces; once it arises, there will be serious trouble. The problem can largely be avoided if they take care to articulate customer needs carefully and then work closely with customers to develop unambiguous functional requirements. They should also recognize that customers are often fickle and should take precautions to avoid being taken by surprise by sudden customer shifts in requirements.

Incorrect Requirements

The needs addressed may be those of the wrong customer, the articulated needs may reflect the biases of the needs articulator, and inherently fuzzy needs may be misinterpreted. In any such cases, functional requirements built on poorly articulated needs will be off the mark. This is a certainty. The final deliverable (assuming the project gets that far) will bear little or no relationship to what the customers need and want.

A large share was dedicated to suggesting ways to carry out the needs recognition and particular tasks effectively, so it is not necessary to rehash the earlier material here, except to offer a summary of steps that should be taken.

First, project planners should recognize the inherent difficulty of articulating needs. Needs tend to be fuzzy; even those holding them generally aren't quite sure what the needs are. Recognition of the difficulty is important, because it encourages the individuals charged with articulation to give this matter the attention it deserves. Too often these individuals rush in with packaged solutions to problems they don't really understand.

Second, project planners should identify the most relevant customers. In most situations, project planners will be dealing with multiple customers, only some of whose needs should be addressed in the project. They should avoid organizing their projects around the needs of peripheral or non relevant customers.

Third, project planners should work closely with customers in articulating their needs. Needs articulation entails a certain amount of hand holding; the needs articulator and the customers should work closely together to hammer out a well-formulated and accurate statement of what it is the customers need.

Fourth, project planners should be aware of the most common pitfalls associated with needs articulation. They should avoid gold-plating needs (that is, offering customers more than they need), imposing their own needs on customers, and assuming a paternalistic, father knows-best attitude in dealing with customers.

Imprecise and Ambiguous Requirements

A major problem arises when requirements are posited in such a way that they are imprecise and ambiguous, subject to different interpretations of their meaning. Imprecise requirements are invitations to problems. When requirements are ambiguously specified, two people can look at the same statement and disagree on what it means. The disagreement can become vehement, since it is clear to each party what the specification is saying, and the fact that the other party does not view the specification "correctly" is attributed to obstinacy, stupidity, or outright dishonesty.

There are various reasons that requirements are specified imprecisely. Some of these reasons are legitimate and understandable. Others reflect sloppy thinking, impatience, or a conscious desire to obfuscate things. Following are some the more obvious reasons for the imprecise specification of requirements.

Nature of Human Language

Human language is naturally ambiguous. While this ambiguity makes for interesting poetry, it is not well suited to describing the requirements of project deliverables. For example, we may specify that we want to furnish our waiting room with chairs that are fire-engine red. For most people, this immediately conjures up an image of a bright red color. But there are many varieties of bright red. (Of course, we could go to our local fire department to get a better idea of what fire engine red is, but this would not be very useful in my neighborhood, where the fire trucks are yellow.) We can be more precise in specifying our color if we request a particular upholstery fabric using its color identification number, or if we attach to the requirements statement a sample of the desired color. If we want to carry this matter of precision even further, we can describe the color according to its wavelength in the visible light spectrum.

This discussion points out the difficulty of depending on human language to describe requirements. For requirements to be precise, we must often supplement our verbal descriptions with additional supporting material: drawings, samples, maps, photographs, and technical data, for example. We can reduce the imprecision in the verbal portion of the requirements statement by describing what we want in excruciating detail, leaving nothing to the imagination. In this last instance, however, we run the risk of overwhelming project staff with impenetrable verbiage that they may choose to ignore.

Deliberate Imprecision for Flexibility

Sometimes requirements are stated ambiguously on purpose, simply to maintain flexibility in the project. This approach is common in state-of-the-art projects, on which there is generally great uncertainty about how the project will proceed. The fear is that the precise statement of requirements will constrict project staff in their work, discouraging them from exploiting unanticipated opportunities as they arise.

Deliberate imprecision is also common in projects that are filled with conditional outcomes. These are projects on which when asked, "What is it that you want?" a customer responds, "It depends on how things work out." The danger with this approach is that the project may drift aimlessly. As a consequence, it runs the risk of never being concluded or of producing a deliverable that meets no one's needs. This is precisely the outcome of many basic research projects.

Human Conflict Preventing Consensus

When people cannot achieve a consensus on what it is that should emerge from a project, they may be unable to generate clear-cut requirements. They may postpone hard choices until later, hoping that the conflict among them will be resolved and things will somehow straighten themselves out. What is likely to happen is that the loosely phrased requirements will take on a life of their own and lead to a deliverable that satisfies none of the contending parties.

Given the tendency of poorly formulated requirements to cause project troubles, it is usually better to make the hard choices as early as possible in the project life cycle. These choices will have to be reckoned with some day; if they are addressed later in the project and it is determined that the project has been moving in the wrong direction, the consequences for the budget and schedule may be devastating.

Inherently Nebulous Information Age Projects

Information age projects often deal with intangibles or "semitangibles," whereas traditional projects in construction and engineering deal with things you can touch and readily see. For example, someone who is designing a project to carry out a marketing study is dealing primarily with abstractions consumers, consumer preferences, hypothetical product prices, potential competitors, mythical competing products, and so forth. Trying to get a firm grip on these abstractions is something like trying to grab a handful of sand.

Seasoned professionals who spend their lives working with intangibles develop the capacity to "see" what the end product will look like, just as a draftsperson can look at a blank sheet of paper and "see" the drawing that will ultimately emerge. The problem is that customers are generally not seasoned professionals accustomed, say, to designing on-line information systems or undertaking sophisticated marketing studies. In trying to visualize the deliverable, they cannot see anything but an amorphous blob. Only as the project evolves and takes shape do they begin to have an inkling of what is being developed. Now that they can see what is emerging, they may not like it and may demand that the project take a different turn to produce something that is more to their liking. This is a very common occurrence with projects dealing with intangibles and semitangibles.

What project staff must do to minimize problems created by the inherently ethereal nature of their projects is to help customers "see" the results of the project as early as possible. They should make frequent use of visual tools, such as drawings, flow diagrams, and tables, and they can do what architects and engineers regularly do in their projects: create simple prototypes of the deliverable, which they can show to the customers. Rather than build a physical model of a building or an airplane, they might put together simple back of-the-envelope mock-ups of the thing they are developing a scaled down computerized accounting system or a sample market study, for example.

Customers' Lack of Expertise. Everybody knows that an expert is someone who is very good at doing something. A tennis expert is good at playing tennis, a computer expert is good at writing code, a legal expert is good at interpreting the law, and so forth. By the same token, someone who is not an expert will find it difficult to do these things well. Customers are generally not experts with regard to the technical content of the projects carried out to meet their needs. They may have expertise in other areas, but this other expertise may be only marginally helpful to them in formulating needs and requirements for their project.

Albert Einstein was a brilliant theoretical physicist of international renown. To my generation children during Einstein's last years his name is virtually synonymous with the word *genius*. Yet I doubt if Einstein would have been very effective in describing the precise requirements of an accounting system to help Princeton's Institute for Advanced Studies (his employer) keep better track of how he and his colleagues spent their research funds.

One important task of the project team is to educate customers about relevant features of the potential deliverable. Certainly, customers cannot be expected to know everything, but just how well educated should they be? This is difficult to answer specifically. There are dangers with both overeducation and undereducation. If too much effort is devoted to educating customers, they may be overwhelmed with detail that they cannot and possibly don't want to understand. In this case, the well-meaning attempt at customer education may produce a completely opposite result. Feeling themselves lost in a miasma of incomprehensible technicalities, customers may withdraw from the process and leave the project definition in the hands of the experts. These experts unfortunately often have little understanding of what the customers will ultimately find acceptable.

But if little or no effort is devoted to educating customers, they will not know enough to be useful partners in the project definition process. Their input will be ill informed and may steer the project into fruitless side excursions. Ultimately, a deliverable will be produced that will not be very useful to them.

Project staff should be sensitive to this issue. The temptation is to ignore customer education altogether and possibly even to intimidate the customers with expertise. Let's face it: customers can be a big pain. They don't know what they want or what is good for them, yet this doesn't stop them from telling project staff how to do their job. When customers timidly offer suggestions, experts who really don't want customer kibitzing often react by overwhelming them with terms and statistics beyond their ken, hoping to intimidate them with a technical whirlwind. Perhaps this tactic gains some momentary peace for the project staff, but in the long run, it may lead to the creation of deliverables that customers do not want.

How much should customers know? In general, they should know enough to be able to contribute meaningfully to the needs articulation and requirements specification efforts. They should also know enough so that they are not surprised with the final outcome. The specific amount of education that should be directed at them has to be determined on a case-by-case basis.

Oversights on the Part of Project Planners. The final reason that requirements are stated imprecisely is more pedestrian than the others. Simply put, this may happen because of sheer oversight, reflecting unstated assumptions or an incomplete understanding of what the project should entail and what the deliverable should be. In asking the painter in the example to paint our office pale blue, we may exclude the requirement to keep the ceiling white because it does not occur to us that this is an issue.

These kinds of oversights occur on all but the most routine projects. There is a certain inevitability to them. They occur because we operate according to unstated assumptions and because we are not omniscient, lacking sufficient imagination to identify every possible meaningful contingency that our project should address.

One way to minimize such oversights is to go to those who will actually carry out the assigned tasks and ask them what kinds of contingencies might arise that should be dealt with in the project specifications. A good long-run approach for dealing with such oversights is to compile a project-by-project checklist of requirements that should be addressed on all projects. As more and more project experience is gained, the list will grow in depth and breadth. Workers in the construction industry are familiar with this kind of list.

Shifting Requirements

The third and final broad area of requirements-related problems focuses on problems associated with shifting requirements. Projects are dynamic things, so it should not come as a surprise that there are strong pressures to modify the original requirements as a project evolves. However, modification may play havoc with the project plan, which is built on specified requirements and may lead to cost and schedule overruns.

Four common situations resulting in changes in requirements are illustrated in the following cases:

Buyer's Remorse: Maureen Shea is the chief administrator of Marvin Gelb Memorial Hospital. This hospital is overcrowded, with three patients typically occupying a single room. Shea and her staff have long entertained a dream of building a new wing on the hospital, which would dramatically ameliorate the condition. When a three-point plunge in mortgage rates occurs, Dr. Shea seizes the opportunity and enters into a contract with a construction firm to build the new wing. It will accommodate 120 beds, a major addition to the patient-handling capability of the hospital.

No sooner is the contract with the builder signed than Shea reads in the local paper a series of articles on the growing popularity of inexpensive outpatient care facilities in the region. She begins to worry that perhaps she has bitten off more than she can chew with her expansion of the hospital. Five months into the project, after the foundation has been poured and the skeleton of the new wing has risen from the ground, Shea begins discussions with the builder to revise the construction plans so that the facility will accommodate only 60 new beds instead of the original 120. She is shocked to learn that this 50 percent reduction in the wing's capacity will save only 15 percent in construction charges.

This case illustrates a phenomenon that real estate agents and car dealers are familiar with. It is so common in these lines of business that it has been given a name: buyer's remorse. It is also common in project management, especially with controversial or high-risk projects.

After much thought and debate, a decision is made to launch a costly project, and no sooner is the decision made than those responsible for it have second thoughts. They may now try to scale down or even eliminate the project in order to reduce some of the deleterious consequences they imagine will hit them if the project does not work out as expected.

This scaling down may be very costly, especially if the project is well under way, since it entails major changes in the original project plan. When this situation arises, the project manager must make it clear to the customers that changes to the plan will be expensive.

Insurmountable Obstacles: Marsha Bronfman is a graduate student working on her doctoral dissertation, which focuses on the public health problems of a developing country. Central to her study is a questionnaire survey of public health practitioners in the country, designed to identify major obstacles to establishing an effective public health program there. She spends two months developing and testing the questionnaire. When it is ready, she sends out 350 copies to the principal public health workers in the country.

A few days later, she receives a visit from an official of the ministry of health, telling her that she had no authority to conduct the survey and that she is forbidden to do further work on it. Bronfman suddenly finds herself persona non grata in the country. What is worse from her perspective is that her doctoral dissertation is jeopardized, since it was designed to focus on the results of the survey analysis. If she is going to complete her dissertation, she will have to revise her research strategy completely.

The sudden appearance of insurmountable obstacles, such as those Bronfman encountered, is a common experience on projects. Any project that blazes new trails runs a strong risk of encountering such obstacles. With technical projects, for example, we are almost assured that technical glitches will force us to utter that age-old expostulation, "Well, I guess it's back to the drawing board!"

Flights of Fancy: Brian Davis and his design team are developing a new toaster for Appliance Masters Co. They spend two weeks working closely with Daniel Seligman, vice president of new product development. Seligman is a highly creative individual the classic idea man and he offers several novel suggestions for features that should be built into the new toaster. Davis accepts the suggestions and begins building a prototype of the new toaster.

Two months later, Seligman visits the design shop to see how the toaster is progressing. Viewing the nearly finished prototype, he becomes quite excited. "I've just had a brainstorm, " he exclaims. "Let's include a voice synthesizer chip in the toaster, enabling the toaster to 'talk' to the user." The design team members, recognizing that this suggestion would require a major redesign of the product, look at Brian Davis with apprehension. "We'll do it, " says Davis, and the design team members groan inwardly.

Three months later, Seligman returns to the design shop to review the nearly completed prototype of the talking toaster. The demonstration he sees causes him to jump with glee. "This is great, " he says. "This is the stuff of science fiction! You know, we should carry the toaster one step further than we have. What we produce should not be a mere toaster; it should be an information center, the brains for all kitchen appliances. Look into this, will you, Brian?" Brian nods his head in agreement while performing some lightning calculations in his head. The latest request will extend the project by at least nine months and will require doubling the design team.

Seligman's vision of the toaster's possibilities evolved with the physical development of the toaster itself. As the new toaster took on tangible shape, Seligman's imagination was stimulated to come up with new possibilities. Such a phenomenon is common on projects. Although suggested changes in the project requirements may ultimately lead to a superior product, they can create serious problems for the project manager.

Changes in the requirements are not cost free. Because of them, schedules may be stretched out, costs may escalate, and other projects in the queue may have to be postponed or canceled. If changes are constantly being required, the project also runs the serious risk of never being completed.

Seizing Opportunities: Nancy and David Rama buy a run-down old house with a view to refurbishing it and renting it out. They hire a contractor to carry out cosmetic improvements. Because the house is structurally sound, the contractor's efforts are largely dedicated to stripping off old paint, removing wallpaper, plastering cracks in walls and ceilings, repainting, and refinishing the hardwood floors.

While removing paint from the mantel of the living room fireplace, the contractor discovers that the wood under the paint is beautiful hand-carved chestnut. Similarly, he finds that the banister leading down the stairs is hand-carved chestnut. As more paint is removed from window frames, it becomes clear that the Ramas have bought a quality house. Consequently, they change their original plans and decide to undertake a major renovation, which will entail far more cost and effort than initially planned. They figure that the $50,000 renovation cost will enhance the value of the house by $80,000, so the added expenditure seems worthwhile.

This case is similar in many respects to the previous one; Seligman too no doubt saw himself as seizing opportunities that presented themselves to him. The line separating flights of fancy from seized opportunities can be thin.

There is an important difference between the two, however. Flights of fancy typically entail an undisciplined impulse to change requirements without regard for cost, schedule, or resources. Habitual practitioners of this "method" of project development substitute their ad hoc approach for sound project planning. In effect, they are proponents of the plan-as-you-go school of project management. The impact of this approach on project budgets and schedules can be devastating.

Seizing opportunities, in contrast, involves a measured response to unanticipated project developments. It entails capitalizing on the unexpected. For this to be successful, it must be determined that the benefits of changing requirements outweigh the costs.

Each of these four cases illustrates how easy and natural it is for requirements to change. Sometimes change is for the better and will result in improved project output. At other times, change is merely disruptive and results in delays and unwise increases in costs. Project staff can count on changes in the specification of requirements, and they must learn to identify such changes as they occur. This is not always easy. Changes in requirements can be subtle and can occur very gradually, almost imperceptibly.

Once professional staff have identified possible changes, they must learn to anticipate the consequences of these changes. If the consequences are strongly negative, they must alert their customers to this fact, particularly if the customers are the cause of the disruptive change. Without a conscious methodology for dealing with changes in the specification of requirements, project staff will be only marginally in control of their project.

Fundamental Trade-Off in Specifying Requirements

There is a frustrating built-in conflict facing individuals charged with specifying requirements for a project. On the one hand, they might be wise to specify everything in detail. Their motto might be, "Leave nothing to chance." Not only might they describe the requirements in great detail, but they could give an item-by-item directive on how the requirements should be achieved. The theory here is that when project managers focus on minutiae and provide detailed instructions on all the steps that have to be carried out to meet specified requirements, there is little likelihood that project staff will interpret requirements incorrectly. In addition, the painstaking enumeration of detail will protect the project performers from potential accusations by customers that they did not do what they said they would.

On the other hand, project planners might be wise to keep things as flexible as possible, so that the project can readily respond to changes in the environment that may require changes in requirements. This more flexible approach is based on the premise that circumstances are bound to arise that will cause alterations in the specifications of requirements.

Problems with Over specification of Requirements

Each of the two approaches outlined above has problems associated with it. Let us begin by addressing problems with the first approach.

Insufficient Information. It is unlikely that individuals specifying requirements will have enough information to plan everything in detail because they cannot know everything that might happen. Detailed specification of requirements puts a tremendous burden on requirements analysts. Remember that they do their work before the deliverable is produced. If they really don't want to leave anything to chance, they need detailed knowledge of all the contingencies that may arise during the course of project implementation, so that they can specify different courses of action for these contingencies.

In practice, individuals writing project requirements are far from omniscient. Even the most carefully specified requirements will be based on guesswork. To the extent that these guesses are off the mark, the specified requirements may or may not be viable or relevant to the needs of the customers.

Initiative Discouraged. Too much detail by the planners tends to discourage initiative on the part of project staff. When all the details of the requirements are spelled out for them, staff members charged with implementing the plan are being told, in effect, not to take any initiative on the project: "We know best what it is you should be producing, so please don't deviate from the specs."

This approach carries with it at least two possible negative consequences. One is that creativity on the part of project staff will be discouraged. Even if they see a way to enhance the deliverable, or if by a change of procedures they can effect time and cost savings, they are discouraged from conveying their insights to their bosses. It is unlikely that truly creative workers would be attracted to such projects.

A second possible negative consequence is that if following the specs becomes the most significant guiding principle of a project, people will be discouraged from assuming responsibility for doing the best job they can. Responsibility is narrowed to a simple directive: meet the specs. If project staff see a fundamental flaw in the specs, they can say, "That's not our problem. We've been told to meet the specs without questioning them, and meet them we will."

Requirements Ignored. Excessive detail in specified requirements often results in project staff ignoring them. A leave-nothing-to-chance philosophy may ultimately backfire on the requirements analyst, creating exactly the opposite effect from what was intended. Too much detail may overwhelm those charged with implementing the project. If much of the detailed material deals with relatively obvious points, there is a temptation on the part of project staff to skim over the minutiae. If the mass of detail is too difficult to digest, project staff may prefer to work things out on their own. Anyone who has tried to put together a model airplane from a kit knows what I am talking about. At the outset, you have every intention of following the instructions carefully, but after five minutes of reading very obvious material, you decide to skip over the simple stuff. You begin painting parts and gluing them together, using the picture on the box as a guide. Occasionally you look at the assembly diagrams, but you are bewildered by the array of code letters, lines, and curves; besides, many of the parts shown in the diagrams don't look like anything you have in your kit. In the end, you have a finished product that looks reasonably similar to the airplane pictured on the box, but there are three or four remaining parts lying on the table that you never incorporated into the model airplane.

Costly Rework Efforts. Excessive rigidity in the specification of requirements may lead to costly rework efforts. Change *will* occur on projects. Perhaps customer needs shift, or new technological developments make the deliverable obsolete in its present form, or a new labor contract escalates the salaries of project staff higher than anticipated. The details will differ from project to project, but the fact remains that *change will occur,* and this change will require rethinking the requirements. If requirements are rigid and deviations from them are prohibited, chances are that at some point, our refusal to accommodate change will catch up with us.

For example, it may become clear early in the project life cycle that meeting a particular requirement is technically unfeasible. However, owing to the rigidity of our approach to requirements, we may proceed as if there were no problem. Ultimately, we come face to face with the fact that the spec is unachievable in its present form. We have no choice but to change our requirements and redo the work we have completed. At this point, the rework effort will be quite expensive. We could have saved considerable time and money had we altered the specified requirements earlier in the project, when we first perceived the problem.

Problems with Excessive Flexibility

Excessive flexibility in specifying requirements also has problems associated with it.

Patchwork Deliverables. The specify-as-you-go approach to defining requirements can easily yield a deliverable that lacks cohesiveness. With such an approach, the deliverable is a patchwork, reflecting many ad hoc decisions rather than a comprehensive vision. To paraphrase a well-known epigram, a camel is a horse designed as a result of the ad hoc specification of requirements.

Chaotic Project Planning. Excessive flexibility will result in chaotic project planning. Planning is the process of identifying how to achieve the requirements, given the constraints of limited time and resources. If requirements are ill defined and evolve willy-nilly over the life of the project, our planning efforts will be chaotic. We will have no cohesive plan; rather, we will have many different plans that change in character as changes are made in the requirements.

Time and Cost Overruns. The previous two problems associated with excessive flexibility are likely to result in time and cost overruns. A patchwork deliverable that does not meet customer needs, for example, may result in rejection of the deliverable by the customers and may give rise to demands to redo the project. Clearly, a project that entails rework efforts will pose both time and budget slippages.

If excessive flexibility causes chaotic planning, this will lead to major inefficiencies in the implementation of the project. We will face false starts and about-faces. Resource utilization will be haphazard, since we will never be quite sure what resources and how many we should be using at any given time. With such inefficiencies, it is unlikely that we will meet our original budget and schedule targets.

Seeking a Middle Ground Approach

We see, then, that the two extremes for specifying requirements will probably yield serious problems for project staff. In specifying requirements, therefore, we should seek some middle ground an approach that avoids the rigidity of immoderately detailed, inflexible requirements, on the one hand, and the chaos of excessively free-form requirements, on the other. To put this in a more positive light, we want requirements that are firm and clear enough to avoid problems of ambiguity and volatility and at the same time sufficiently flexible to accommodate changes that are bound to occur during the course of a project.

General Guidelines for Specifying Requirements

I cannot overstate the observation that along with inadequately articulated customer needs, poorly formulated requirements stand out as an enormously significant source of grief on projects. If the requirements are stipulated incorrectly, or are subject to multiple interpretations, or are too complicated, or are forever changing, the whole project suffers.

The good news is that many of the problems associated with requirements specification can be minimized if those involved with projects project staff and customers alike pay attention to some basic guidelines:

Rule 1: State the requirement explicitly and have project staff and customers sign off on it. Too often, especially on small, informal projects, requirements are implied rather than stated explicitly. For example, George says to Martha, "Write up a proposal to bid on that Molsen job, will you?" Martha agrees, and four days later she turns in a document that George finds to be too short, lacking in methodological rigor, and emphasizing the wrong issues. George calls Martha in and chews her out. "This isn't what I asked for, " he chides, pointing out its various shortcomings to Martha in detail.

Two features of this incident stand out. First, it is ludicrous for George to say, "This isn't what I asked for, " since he never really did say what it was that he wanted. *Of course,* what Martha delivered was not what George asked for. This was ensured by the fact that George never conveyed anything but the vaguest sense of his requirements. A second interesting feature is this: only after the project has failed from George's perspective does he sit down and elucidate what he expects out of the Molsen proposal. That is, in pointing out the problems with the proposal, he is hinting at what his requirements are ex post facto. Even here he is *implying* his requirements rather than stating them explicitly and systematically.

In general, it is a good idea to be explicit in stating requirements. The explicit listing of requirements can be viewed as a contract, focusing on what the customers want and what project staff have agreed to deliver. As with any contract linking customers and producer, it is wise to have both parties carefully review the stated requirements and, if the requirements are acceptable, to sign off on them.

Rule 2: Be realistic; assume that if a requirement can be misinterpreted, it will be misinterpreted. This rule is a variant of Murphy's Law, which states that if something can go wrong, it will. In examining the way a requirement is stated, do everything possible to determine how it can be misinterpreted. Ask different staff members to offer their interpretations of the requirement. Ask customers their interpretation. Determine the views of other people who will be affected by the project; if their opinion of what the requirement should be varies from the customers' opinion, there may be trouble. If it is an important project, hire independent experts to review the requirements and see whether their viewpoints correspond with yours. If these things are done early in the project, you are likely to avoid some nasty surprises midway through or at the end.

Rule 3: Be realistic; recognize that there will be changes on your project and that things will not go precisely as anticipated. The basic lesson here is to avoid excessive rigidity in formulating requirements and to anticipate change.

Rule 4: To as great an extent as possible, include pictures, graphs, physical models, and other nonverbal exhibits in the formulation of requirements. I had my first lesson on the limitations of language when I was a sixth-grade student. One day the school principal visited my class and set us a challenge: to describe a spiral verbally, without using our hands. I think we did a pretty good job of it, but it was difficult. We would have done a better job if we could have simply drawn a spiral on the blackboard.

This lesson was driven home to me a couple of years ago when I carried out a study on how patent examiners determine the technical capabilities of the inventions they review. I interviewed a number of patent examiners, and over and over they told me that the key to doing their job was to review the drawings that accompany the verbal description of the invention. Several said that a review of the drawings alone gives them almost full knowledge of what an invention can do and what the patent applicant's patent claims are.

The point here is an old one: a picture or graph, or flowchart, or mock-up model is worth a thousand words. Engineers and architects have long recognized this; the clarification of requirements with blueprints, drawings, and the like is commonplace in these professions. It is less commonplace in fact, downright rare in the more mundane, informal, white-collar projects we typically carry out in our organizations. This is a pity, since these nonverbal exhibits can dramatically sharpen the clarity of the requirements we are trying to establish.

Rule 5: Establish a system to monitor carefully any changes made to the requirements. Construction companies have long recognized that they would go broke if they did not keep meticulous records of changes made to their projects, and so they have established systems to keep track of them. Systems developed for keeping track of changes should address two basic issues. First, projects are themselves systems that is, they are made up of interrelated parts. If a change is made to one part, will it have system wide ripple effects? Remember that the consequences of a single change may be profound and widespread.

The second basic issue is that changes have costs associated with them. The costs may be obvious, as when a change requires the disassembly of a piece of hardware and its reassembly in a new way. But the costs may also be more subtle. For example, change always has hidden administrative costs associated with it.

There is a strong relationship between these two issues. The greater is the system wide impact of a change, the greater is the likelihood that costs associated with the change will be substantial.

The nature of the system developed for tracking changes to project requirements will vary according to the character of the project and the organization in which it is carried out. Large, complex projects require a high degree of formality in tracking changes; otherwise, countless small changes will be lost in the shuffle. The dominant approach to managing change on large projects, called *configuration management,* requires detailed documentation of all actions associated with change requests. With smaller projects, formality can be reduced. In fact, too much paperwork can measurably decrease the productivity of the smaller effort.

However, at a minimum, in large projects and small, written change orders should be required. The change order should contain the following information:

- Date of the change request
- Name of the person requesting the change
- Description of the change
- Statement of the change's impact on the project
- Listing of tasks and staff affected by the change
- Estimate of the cost of the change
- Signature of the individual making the change request, indicating that this individual is aware of the cost and performance impacts of the requested change

With such a written change order, those desiring changes whether designers or customers are required to take responsibility for their requests. Given this personal assumption of responsibility, they are less likely to make frivolous requests that may have serious impacts.

Rule 6: Educate project staff and customers to the problems of specifying requirements. Anyone experienced in working with projects recognizes that one important cause of problems is that inexperienced staff and naive customers are ignorant of what is involved in generating and meeting project requirements. They demonstrate time and again the old maxim that fools rush in where angels fear to tread. Customers may pepper the project team with requests for changes, not realizing the enormous impact these requests may have. Staff may set up requirements in an arbitrary, slipshod way, seeing them more as guidelines for action than as blueprints that need to be followed precisely. The list of mischief that staff and customers can get into unwittingly is never ending.

Rapid Prototyping

Rapid prototyping, a project management technique that emerged in the software industry in the 1980s, recognizes that with computer software projects or any other projects that deal largely with intangibles it is hard to picture concretely what the project should be producing. Consequently, there is a good chance that the final deliverable, based on an amorphous understanding of customer needs, will not satisfy the customers.

To deal with this reality, rapid prototyping allows for the dynamic development of requirements rather than demanding that all requirements be cast in iron at the outset of the project. It allows the customers to play an active role in defining the requirements as the project is being carried out. It is, in effect, a method built on a partnership between customer and developer.

At the heart of the technique is the concept of iterative prototyping of an intangible deliverable. Let's say that a software development team is contracted to produce a computerized inventory control system. Working closely with the customers, the team identifies needs and from these generates requirements. Then the team begins work on the project, with the objective of quickly putting together a simple prototype of the final deliverable.

The first prototype may be nothing more than a set of computer screen images of a data entry form. When the prototype is completed, it is brought before a panel of customers to provide them an opportunity to see what is being developed early in the project life cycle. After examining the prototype, the customers may, for example, express general satisfaction with the product but note that it appears that the emerging system will not process and track incoming inventory items well.

The software team then takes account of the customers' input, refines the software, and quickly develops a new, more detailed prototype. Once again, the customer panel examines the prototype and offers comments and suggestions. This and subsequent reviews can take hours or days, depending on the nature of the project. At a certain point, they actually drive the evolving prototype using test data, thereby developing a good sense of the capabilities of the emerging system. The project proceeds in this iterative fashion until a well-defined prototype is developed.

On small systems, the final approved prototype might be handed over to the customers as a functioning system. On more complex systems, the final prototype is given to requirements experts, who review it to see what customer needs and wants are embedded in it. With this information, they specify customer-focused requirements carefully, and these well-specified requirements are used to design and build a product that leads to high levels of customer satisfaction.

For rapid prototyping to work effectively, rules for prototyping and requesting improvements to the evolving system must be carefully spelled out; otherwise, the project may never be brought to a conclusion, and costs may get out of hand. For example, how detailed should a prototype be? How many rounds of prototypes should be developed during the course of the project? What are the limitations on customer requests for improvements to the deliverable? How will the cost impacts of changes to the prototype be calculated?

The advantage of the prototyping approach is obvious. The final deliverable should make the customers happy, because they played a major role in defining what it looks like and does. This is not a trivial point, since costly rework efforts will have to be undertaken if the deliverable is unsatisfactory, and the project may even have to be redone completely. Another advantage is that rapid prototyping provides project professionals with a methodology for making the intangible a bit more tangible for dealing proactively with some of the significant problems that arise on amorphous, white-collar, information age projects.

The disadvantages of rapid prototyping are also obvious. For one thing, there is a risk that heavy involvement of the customers in defining the product as it evolves will be taken as an invitation to make changes according to whim. Consequently, rapid prototyping efforts should employ conscious change control processes. There is also a danger that unless there is a strong commitment on the part of both the customers and project staff to bring the project to a conclusion, the project may drift from prototype to prototype without ever coming to closure.

Summary

Writing good requirements is a formidable task. The pitfalls are bountiful: the requirements may be ambiguous or unrealistic, or they may have no bearing on the customers' true needs. They may be too detailed or not detailed enough. They may be too rigid or overly flexible. If the pitfalls are not avoided, problems will arise.

This chapter has shown that there are many ways that project staff can develop good requirements. The single most important step is the simplest: be aware of the role that requirements play in the evolution of a project. Staff should recognize that requirements form the basis of project plans, since the purpose of the plans is to describe how the requirements can be met. If the requirements are deficient, the project plan is flawed, and if the plan is flawed, its implementation is defective. An understanding of the connection between requirements and the plan also leads to an appreciation of how modifications to the requirements can yield cost and schedule overruns, since changes in the requirements necessitate changes in the plan.

With a thorough understanding of the importance of requirements, staff will be better able to identify and deal with the many big and little requirements-related problems that inevitably arise on their project.

BIBLIOGRAPHY

Adrian James J., *Quantitative Methods in Construction Management*, Elsevier Publishing Co., New York, 1973.

Afiesimama Boma T., "Aggregate Manpower Requirements for Strategic Project Planning," *Computers and Industrial Engineering*, Vol. 12, No. 4, 1987, pp. 249-262.

Akao Y. and T. Asaka, eds., *Quality Function Deployment*, Productivity, Inc., Cambridge,. MA, 1990.

Badiru Adedeji B., "Computational Survey of Univariate and Multivariate Learning Curve Models," *IEEE Transactions on Engineering Management*, Vol. 39, No. 2, May 1992b, pp. 176-188.

Badiru Adedeji B., *Expert Systems Applications in Engineering and Manufacturing*, Prentice-Hall, Englewood Cliffs, NJ, 1992a.

Badiru Adedeji B., *Project Management Tools for Engineering and Management Professionals*, Industrial Engineering and Management Press, Norcross, GA, 1991a.

Camm Jeffrey D., James R. Evans, and Norman K. Womer, *"The Unit Learning Curve Approximation of Total Cost," Computers and Industrial Engineering*, Vol. 12, No. 3, 1987, pp. 205-213.

Canada John R. and William G. Sullivan, *Economic and multiattribute Evaluation of Advanced Manufacturing Systems*, Prentice-Hall, Englewood Cliffs, NJ, 1989.

Carraway Robert L. and R. L. Schmidt, "An Improved Discrete Dynamic Programming Algorithm for Allocating

Resources Among Interdependent Projects," *Management Science*, Vol. 37, No. 9, 1991, pp. 1195-1200.

Chapman C. B., "The Optimal Allocation of Resources to a Variable Timetable," *Operational Research Quarterly*, Vol. 21, No. 1, March 1970, pp. 81-90.

Dallenback H. and J. George, Introduction to Operations Research Techniques, Allyn and Bacon, Inc., Boston, 1978.

Dantzig George B., Linear Programming and Extensions, Princeton University Press, Princeton, NJ, 1963.

Dar-El E. M. and Yigal Tur, "A Multi-Resource Project Scheduling Algorithm," AIIE Transactions, Vol. 9, March 1977, pp. 44-52.

East E. William and Jeffrey G. Kirby, A Guide to Computerized Project Scheduling, Van Nostrand Reinhold, New York, 1989.

Elmaghraby Salah E. and Willy S. Herroelen, "On The Measurement of Complexity in Activity Networks," European Journal of Operations Research, Vol. 5, 1980, pp. 223-234.

Elmaghraby Salah E., Activity Networks: Project Planning and Control by Network Models, John Wiley & Sons, New York, 1977.

Fabrycky Wolter J. and B. S. Blanchard, Life-Cycle Cost and Economic Analysis, Prentice-Hall, Englewood Cliffs, NJ, 1991.

Farid Foad and R. Kangari, "A Knowledge-Based System for Selecting Project Management Microsoftware Packages," Project Management Journal, Vol. 22, No. 3, 1991, pp. 55-61.

Gallagher C., "A Note on PERT Assumptions," Management Science, Vol. 33, 1987, p. 1360.

Gessner Robert A., Manufacturing Information Systems: Implementation Planning, John Wiley & Sons, New York, 1984.

Gibson John E., Modern Management of the High-Technology Enterprise, Prentice-Hall, Englewood Cliffs, NJ, 1990.

Hajek V. G., Management of Engineering Projects, McGraw-Hill, New York, 1977.

Hajek Victor G., Project Engineering: Profitable Technical Program Management, McGraw-Hill, New York, 1965.

Ignizio J. P., Goal Programming and Extensions, D. C. Heath and Company, Lexington, MA, 1976.

Izuchukwu John I., "Shortening the Critical Path," Mechanical Engineering, February 1990, pp. 59-60.

Jelen Frederic C. and James H. Black, Cost and Optimization Engineering, McGraw-Hill, New York, 1983.

Jennett Eric, "Guidelines for Successful Project Management," Chemical Engineering, July 1973, pp. 70-82.

Kaimann R. A., "Coefficient of Network Complexity," Management Science, Vol. 21, No. 2, 1974, pp. 172-177.

Kaimann R. A., "Coefficient of Network Complexity: Erratum," Management Science, Vol. 21, No. 10, 1975, pp. 1211-1212.

Lapin L., QuickQuant+: Decision Making Software, Alamo Publishing Company, Pleasanton, CA, 1991.

Lapin L., Statistics for Modern Business Decisions, 2ed, Harcourt Brace Jovanovich, New York, 1978.

MacCrimmon Kenneth R. and Charles A. Ryavec, "An Analytical Study of the PERT Assumptions," Operations Research, Vol. 12, 1964, pp. 16-21.

Machina M. J., "Decision-Making in the Presence of Risk," Science, Vol. 236, May 1987, pp. 537-543.

Nanda Ravinder, "Using Learning Curves in Integration of Production Resources," Proceedings of 1979 IIE Fall Conference, 1979, pp. 376-380.

Navon Ronie, "Financial Planning in a Project-Oriented Industry," Project Management Journal, Vol. 21, No. 1, 1990, pp. 43-48.

O'Brien James J., CPM in Construction Management, 3ed, McGraw-Hill, New York, 1984.

Patterson J. H., "Comparison of Exact Approaches for Solving Multiconstrained Resource Project Scheduling," Management Science, Vol. 30, No. 7, 1984, pp. 854-867.

Ravindran A., Don T. Phillips, and James J. Solberg, Operations Research: Principles and Practice, 2ed, John Wiley & Sons, New York, 1987.

Reinfeld N. V. and W. R. Vogel, Mathematical Programming, Prentice-Hall, Englewood Cliffs, NJ., 1958.

Saaty Thomas L., "A Scaling Method for Priorities in Hierarchical Structures," Journal of Mathematical Psychology, Vol. 15, June 1977, pp. 235-281.

Saaty Thomas L., The Analytic Hierarchy Process, McGraw-Hill, New York, 1980.

Taguchi Genichi, "Introduction to Quality Engineering: Designing Quality into Products and Processes", Quality Resources, White Plains, NY, 1986.

Villeda R. and B. V. Dean, "On the Optimal Safe Allocation and Scheduling of a Work Force in a Toxic Substance Environment," IEEE Transactions on Engineering Management, Vol. 37, No. 2, 1990, pp. 95-101.

Wagner Harvey M., Principles of Operations Research, Prentice-Hall, Englewood Cliffs, NJ, 1969.

Yelle Louis E., "Adding Life Cycles to Learning Curves," Long Range Planning, Vol. 16, No. 6, December 1983, pp. 82-87.

Yelle Louis E., "The Learning Curve: Historical Review and Comprehensive Survey," Decision Sciences, Vol. 10, No. 2, April 1979, pp. 302-328.

Zaloom Victor, "On the Resource Constrained Project Scheduling Problem," AIIE Transactions, Vol. 3, No. 4, December 1971, pp. 302-305.

INDEX